Berlitz®
India

Original text by Jack Altman
Revised and updated by David Abram
Series Editor: Tony Halliday

Berlitz POCKET GUIDE

India

Fourth Edition 2005
Updated 2007

PHOTOGRAPHY CREDITS
David Abram 12, 64, 65, 103, 104, 120, 126, 146, 183, 210–11; David Abram/Apa 148, 223; Apa Publications 173; AKG London 24, 47, 49; British Library 38; Jerry Dennis 203; Link/Dinodia 15, 18, 63, 67, 69, 74, 96, 99, 107, 117, 124, 128, 133, 141, 157, 164, 168, 180, 191, 200, 205, 218; Getty Images 57; Tony Halliday 6, 23, 79, 83, 84, 85, 91, 108, 109, 110, 113, 118, 122; Blaine Harrington 20, 160–1, 195; Illustrated London News 44; Walter Imber/Apa 155, 26, 28, 31, 32, 37, 50, 71, 73, 86, 88–9, 112, 132, 136, 138–9, 142, 163, 166, 171, 175, 177, 185, 186, 192, 193, 199, 206, 213, 220; India Tourist Board 145; Wilhelm Klein 45; Bob Krist 181; D. Messant 111; Nehru Memorial Museum 52; Abe Nowitz/Apa 134; Panos Pictures 9; Gunter Pfannmuller 178; Princeton Library, NJ 43; Simon Reddy/Alamy 217; Dave Sanger 16; Nicholas Sumner 76–7, 80, 92, 95, 114–5, 121, 131, 158, 188–9, 204; Topham Picturepoint 54, 55; Trip/Dinodia 208; Ubiquitous 60, 197; Victoria & Albert Museum 35; Bill Wassman/Apa 8, 13, 151, 152, 153, 196; Bill Wassman 100; Henry Wilson 11

CONTACTING THE EDITORS
Every effort has been made to provide accurate information in this publication, but changes are inevitable. The publisher cannot be responsible for any resulting loss, inconvenience or injury. We would appreciate it if readers would call our attention to any errors or outdated information by contacting Berlitz Publishing, PO Box 7910, London SE1 1WE, England. Fax: (44) 20 7403 0290; email: berlitz@apaguide.co.uk www.berlitzpublishing.com

Superb frescoes and sculpture adorn the breathtaking cave temples of Ajanta and Ellora (page 135)

Madurai (page 182) is famed for the Meenakshi temple, with its brightly coloured and towering *gopuras*

Buddhist monasteries hug the hills of Ladakh (page 103)

TOP TEN ATTRACTIONS

The palm-lined backwaters of Kerala (page 184) represent tropical India at its most intense ▼

The deserted Vijayanagar capital at Hampi (page 193) is perhaps India's most evocative ruin ◄

The bathing *ghats* of the sacred city of Varanasi (page 88) present an unforgettable spectacle ►

A colonial retreat from summer heat, Darjeeling (page 159) is within sight of the Himalayas ▼

► Agra (page 75), location of the Taj Mahal and other Mughal wonders, including nearby Fatehpur Sikri

Khajuraho (page 142), Hindu temples festooned with erotic sculpture ►

The desert citadel of ► Jaisalmer (page 121) has a golden sandstone fort and wonderful old town houses

CONTENTS

A ➤ in the text denotes a highly recommended sight

Fact Sheets

INDIA AND ITS PEOPLE

No place for the faint-hearted, India is a constant challenge to mind and body, a glorious shock to the system. It is exhilarating, exhausting and infuriating; a land where, you will find, the practicalities of daily life overlay the mysteries of popular myth. In place of the much-publicised, and much-misunderstood, mysticism of its ancient religions, India in reality has quite another miracle to offer in the sheer profusion of its peoples and landscapes.

The country comprises a diamond-shaped subcontinent that stretches over 3,000km (1,800 miles) from the Kashmiri Himalaya in the north right down to Kanyakumari, or Cape Comorin, on the Indian Ocean. From east to west India also covers about 3,000km, from Arunachal Pradesh and Assam on the border with its neighbours China and Myanmar, to the Gujarat coast on the Arabian Sea. The topography extends from the snows of the high Himalayas, to the deserts of Rajasthan, to the lush tropical landscape of Kerala.

Only in more recent post-colonial times did its natural geography exclude the neighbouring countries of Pakistan and Bangladesh, where, for all the hostilities, there's an undeniable cultural affinity with India. The enormity of India itself means there are different and inevitably conflicting regional and sectarian interests. India boasts no less than 18 official languages: Hindi, Urdu, Sanskrit, Sindhi, Bengali, Marathi, Gujarati, Oriya, Punjabi, Assamese, Kashmiri, Malayalam, Konkani and Ladakhi, as well as Kannada, Tamil and Telugu, and English as an Associate-Official language. An estimated 850 languages are in daily use.

The official national language is Hindi, much to the disgust of the Tamils, but it is spoken by far less than the majority, and English, still much used by government and institutions, is spoken by just 5 percent of the people, mostly in the south and larger cities.

The incomparable Taj Mahal, in the morning

One of the first impressions you'll get at the airport in Delhi or Mumbai (Bombay) is the diversity of India's peoples. From green-eyed and sometimes light brown-haired Kashmiris and the Tibetans from Sikkim or Darjeeling, through the Indo-European-speaking peoples of the heartland, right down to dark-skinned Dravidians from southern India, you soon realise there's no such thing as a 'typical' Indian.

India's prehistoric settlers were probably what anthropologists call Proto-Australoids. They have since been joined by Mongols, Aryans, Greeks, Arabs, Turks, Persians and Afghans, while Dutch, British, Portuguese and French have also left their traces.

Landscape and Heritage

The landscape is alternately rich and arid, lush and desolate. The majestic Himalayas in the north make an appropriate home for Shiva, one of the most revered Hindu gods. Kashmir is a beautiful and coveted land of green forest, alpine meadows and lakes,

Rice cultivation near Goa

while the Punjab in the north-west is the fertile centre of the country's Green Revolution, supporting the nation's self-sufficiency in wheat, barley and millet. On the doorstep of this wealth, the Thar Desert of noble Rajasthan heralds the vast Deccan plateau of parched, ruddy granite that dominates the peninsula of southern India.

Jagganath Temple at Puri

Delhi stands at the western end of the Ganges river basin in which India grows much of its rice. Flanked with patches of forest leading up into the foothills of the Himalayas, the flat plain stretches right across to the Bay of Bengal 1,600km (1,000 miles) away, but some areas are kept as nature reserves for the country's wildlife, notably its tigers, leopards and elephants. Bengal's greenery is the threshold to the tea plantations of Darjeeling and Assam.

The rugged southern peninsula is hemmed in by low-lying mountains; the Vindhya and Satpura to the north and the Western and Eastern Ghats running parallel to the coasts. The forested Malabar coast in the west is sown with crops of coconut, betel nut, pepper, cardamom, rubber and cashew nut, which today still tempt ships across the Arabian Sea. Palm trees line the shores all the way around peninsula India, from Mumbai to the Ganges delta.

India's landscape also features man-made architectural treasures, bearing witness to the many great religions and civilisations that have enriched the country; monuments now, after centuries of neglect, preserved by the restoration programme started by the Archaeological Survey of India. The sights are endless: the Hindu *gopura* tower-gates of the south, the temples of Varanasi

(Benares), the cave monasteries of Ajanta and Ellora, the beautiful and erotic sculptures of Khajuraho, the splendid marble palaces, fortresses and mausoleums of the emperors and maharajas in Delhi, Agra and Rajasthan, the colonial government buildings in New Delhi, or the unusual style of the gothic-oriental municipal piles in Mumbai.

People

The cities' *bastis* (shanty-town districts) are often directly in the shadow of the shining skyscrapers, built by the *basti*-dwellers themselves. Here women carry piles of bricks on their heads as gracefully as they would a pitcher of water. The women are also responsible for one other characteristic of the Indian landscape: cow-dung patties which are preserved and kept for fuel and artfully shaped into mounds.

The only constant in this huge landscape is the presence of people themselves. Even in the vast open spaces of the Rajasthan desert or the Deccan plateau of central India, people

---

Some Statistics

India's area of 3,287,263 sq km (1,269,212 sq miles) makes it the seventh-largest country in the world, but it has the world's second-largest population (after China).

Population: 1.1 billion, of whom roughly 72 percent are Indo-European, mostly in the north, 25 percent Dravidian in the south, 3 percent others. Density is 335 people per sq km (867 per sq mile).

Capital: Delhi, pop. 14,000,000.

Major cities: Mumbai (once Bombay), pop. 18,000,000; Kolkata (once Calcutta), pop. 14,000,000; Chennai (once Madras), pop. 7,000,000; Bangalore, pop. 6,100,000; Hyderabad, pop. 6,100,000; Ahmadabad, pop. 5,100,000; Pune, pop. 4,500,000.

Religion: about 82 percent Hindu, 13 percent Muslim, 2.3 percent Christian, 1.94 percent Sikh, 0.76 percent Buddhist, the remainder Jain and others.

The bustle of Delhi's Old City off Chandni Chowk

appear everywhere, a tribesman on camel-back or a lone woman holding her headdress in her teeth to keep out the dust as she carries a huge pitcher of water or a bundle of firewood on her head. If, as the road stretches before you empty and clear right up to the horizon, you can see only one tree, there's a good chance you'll find at least one *sadhu* (holy man) resting in its shade.

The teeming millions living in Delhi, Mumbai and Kolkata have become legendary. They crowd each other into the roadway, bulge out of tiny auto-rickshaws, and perch on top of buses and trains; a family of four or five clings onto a motor-scooter, and a whole school class on one bullock-cart. It is hazardous: buses do topple over, rooftop passengers on trains do occasionally get swept off the top by an overhanging cable, but they accept the risk for the free ride. Rooftoppers aren't in the habit of buying tickets.

Despite impressive economic progress, there remain vast numbers of people living in absolute poverty, particularly in the big cities but also in rural areas. In India poverty is borne with a kind of stoical resignation that some Westerners may find difficult to comprehend.

The jostling may also be an alien concept to many visitors, but it's a way of life in India. And everyone makes way for the cow, sacred to Hindus. The cow has right of way everywhere, whether walking nonchalantly through the centre of a city, or reclining across a new expressway. After a while you may begin to detect something a bit uncanny in the way a cow seems to look around and beyond her immediate surroundings; it's as if she *knows* that she's sacred.

You can't get around it: India is a country where religion is ever-present. Although the constitution of today describes India as a secular state, religion still plays a vital part in everyday life: in its streets as well as in the architecture, sculpture and painting of its great monuments.

Religions of India

Hinduism

More than 80 percent of the population embraces Hinduism, which is more a way of life than a religion; its sacred rituals and observances are only a small part of what good Hindus believe

A *sadhu* (holy man)

makes them good Hindus. Much more than the mystical elements which fascinate and draw so many Westerners here, Hinduism is concerned with the basics of everyday life: birth, work, health, relationships and death, all of this helped along by regular consultations with an astrologer. India's principal religion may therefore owe its popularity to the fact that it offers something for everyone: mysticism

The cow is sacred to Hindus

and metaphysics for scholars, ritual and spectacle for devo-
teees, austerity, sensuality, tranquillity and frenzy.

Building on early indigenous belief systems and the Vedic
teachings of the Indo-Aryans dating from 1300BC, Hinduism
began to take its present form in the 4th century AD, under considerable pressure for a more 'accessible' religion. Popular devotional worship, *bhakti*, with its appeal to a wide range of people,
replaced the sacrifices practised exclusively by the Brahmins.

It is said there are 330 million gods in the Hindu pantheon,
but they might be seen as 330 million facets of a single divinity.
The three most important manifestations of the godhead are
Vishnu, Brahma and Shiva, which are often presented to West-
erners as a trinity, though this is not really comparable to the
Christian concept.

Vishnu is the preserver of the universe; a four-armed god
with mace, conch, discus and lotus, he has many incarnations,
of which the most famous is Krishna, who appears as conquering hero, flute-playing lover or mischievous baby. Vishnu's
wife Lakshmi is goddess of wealth. Brahma is the creator of

the world, self-born (without mother) in the lotus flower which grew from the navel of Vishnu at the beginning of the universe. Shiva is the dancing destroyer-god, wearing a garland of skulls and snakes around both neck and arms. As the god of time and ascetics, he decides the fate of the world. As lord of beasts and king of dance, Shiva is as passionate as Vishnu is serene. Just in case you think you have got it all clear, remember that Shiva preserves through the renewal arising from destruction.

Hindu ethics say that the path to salvation has three principles: righteousness, prosperity honestly achieved and, not least, pleasure. At the centre of the confrontation with the harsh reality of daily life are the concepts of *dharma* and *karma*; that is 'correct' behaviour and the implication that the sum total of one's acts in a previous life will determine one's present station in this and future lives. A better reincarnation is promised to those whose deeds and actions are good in this station. The ultimate goal is spiritual salvation, or *moksha*, a freeing from the cycle of rebirth.

While this teaching has served to sustain the rigid hierarchy of the caste system, it is not so 'fatalistic' as some would have it. The Hindus say we cannot escape our *karma*, but that with good judgment and foresight we can use it to our advantage.

By the 19th century, reformers such as the Bengali Ram Mohan Roy tried to bring Hinduism into line with imported

Spots, Sacred and Secular

With the aid of a small mirror and a graceful arching hand gesture consecrated in temple sculpture all over India, pilgrims use white, yellow or red paste to daub a *tilak*, or *tika*, mark on their forehead, made up of a dot, stripes or triangles, which denote their sect according to whether they are devotees of Vishnu or Shiva.

Women apply red ochre to a parting in their hair to denote their married status. These days many Indian women, whether married or unmarried, wear a spot in the centre of the forehead called a *bindi* in any colour, simply as a cosmetic accessory.

Europeans ideas, but, thankfully, the monkey-god Hanuman and elephant-headed Ganesh are still idolised, and no one denies the sanctity of the cow and all her products: milk, curd, butter and dung. One of the more notorious practices, self-immolation of widows, known as *sati* (some ultra-traditional castes believe that a widow becomes *sati*, a 'virtuous woman,' by climbing onto her husband's funeral pyre), was outlawed by the British in the 19th century and has now almost disappeared.

Even today, the intricate Hindu caste system can play a role in the Indians' choice of job, spouse and political party,

Krishna and Radha

despite the numerous anti-discrimination statutes passed since Independence. *Brahmins*, the priestly caste, fill many of the top posts in the universities and administration; many Indian Army officers can trace their ancestry to the proud *Kshatriya* warrior caste; business is dominated by the merchant or *Vaishya* caste; and *Shudras* till the land. The casteless, formerly dubbed 'untouchables' but now known as Dalits, have greater opportunities to rise on the social scale these days, a few of them becoming captains of industry and even, in the case of K. R. Narayan, President of the country.

Most marriages in India are arranged traditionally with carefully negotiated dowries. While ever more matrimonial advertisements in the weekend editions of *The Times of India* and other newspapers mention 'caste no bar', just as many specify the required caste or insist on a 'wheatish-complexioned' bride while touting a university diploma or an American work permit.

Islam

India would be unrecognisable without the influence of Islam. The great cities of the north, Delhi, Mumbai and Kolkata, have all been shaped to a great degree by their Muslim inhabitants, as has Hyderabad, in the south; and India's most famous monument, the Taj Mahal, was commissioned by Shah Jahan, the Muslim Mughal Emperor. Although Muslim Arab traders had been visiting India since the 7th century, Islam arrived in force in the 12th century. Hindu conversions to Islam were generally made out of hope of social advancement under Muslim rulers rather than by force.

Even after partition of the country in 1947, India has the third-largest Muslim population in the world, after Indonesia and Pakistan. For all Islam's hostility to idolatry, uncompromising monotheism, and opposition to the caste system, the co-existence between Islam and Hinduism in South Asia has historically been remarkably peaceful. The two religious cultures have fed off each other, resulting in a uniquely syncretic Indo-Islamic culture. In many areas it is not uncommon for local Hindus to worship at the tomb of a Muslim saint, and for local Muslims to take part in the celebrations of Hindu festivals. Unfortunately this mutual tolerance is under threat, as fanatics on both sides target each other's places of worship and engage in indiscriminate acts of violence and killing.

At the mosque of the Qutb Minar

Followers of Islam in India are divided into two primary

groups: Sunnis (adherents of the Sunna law expounded by Muhammad's own words and deeds) and Shias (followers of those interpretations proposed by Muhammad's cousin Ali). The five core beliefs and practices of Islam (the so-called 'five pillars') are: that there is no god but Allah, and Muhammad is His Prophet; to pray five times every day; to perform acts of charity; to fast from dawn to dusk throughout the month of Ramadan; and to go on the *Haj*, or pilgrimage to Makkah (Mecca), at least once during the lifetime of the believer.

Sikhism

The most successful attempt to merge the principles of Hinduism and Islam is that of the **Sikhs** ('disciples'). Nanak, their *guru* (teacher), was born a Hindu in 1469 and reared on the egalitarian principles of Islam. He opposed idolatry and the caste system (which was subsequently too strong to resist). From Islam he took the idea of one God, but refused any such specific conception as Allah. He saw God's manifestation, like Hinduism, as being everywhere in the world He created. Nanak was followed by a succession of nine other living gurus. The militancy of the Sikhs came about only after the execution of Guru Tegh Bahadur by the Mughals. His son, Guru Gobind Singh, founded the Khalsa, a committed and baptised group of men and women. The men took the surname Singh, meaning 'Lion' (not all Singhs are Sikhs), the women Kaur, 'lioness'. Members of the Khalsa wear a turban and keep the five K's: *kesha* (uncut hair and beard), *kangha* (comb for their hair), *kara* (steel bracelet), *kacha* (soldier's shorts) and *kirpan* (dagger).

Sikhs comprise just 2 percent of the population. With strongly martial traditions,

> The first five Sikh gurus were all poets, whose work was collected to form the basis of the Sikh holy book, the Adi Granth. There is a tradition that it was Akbar who granted the daughter of the third guru an area of land in Amritsar on which the Sikhs built their temple in 1577.

Sikh in Amritsar

they make up a fiercely competent élite in the Indian Army, but they are also skilled farmers at the spearhead of the Green Revolution in the Punjab, where most of them live.

During the 1980s, militant Sikhs in the Punjab began to forcibly push their campaign for a separate Sikh homeland, Khalistan. The widespread violence culminated in 1984, with the Indian Army's storming of the Sikh's most holy shrine, the Golden Temple in Amritsar. The violation of the shrine incensed many Sikhs, and the Indian Prime Minister Indira Gandhi, widely blamed for the heavy-handed attack, was subsequently assassinated by her Sikh bodyguards.

Buddhism

Buddhism was founded over 2,500 years ago in reaction to Brahmanic orthodoxy, but it practically vanished as an organised religion from the Indian scene by persecution and absorption into the Hindu mainstream. However, it continues to exert influence on India's spiritual and artistic life to the present day, and is practised by inhabitants of Himalayan regions such as Sikkim and

Ladakh, as well as millions of Tibetan refugees who have made their home in the subcontinent.

The Buddha's own life explains his teachings, but the truth is buried in both legend and historical fact. He was born Siddhartha Gautama in a grove of sal trees at Lumbini (just across the Nepalese border) around the year 563BC. His mother, who was queen of the Sakyas, is said to have conceived him after dreaming that a magnificent white elephant holding a lotus flower in his trunk had entered her side. Siddhartha grew up in princely luxury, but when he was taken out one day to the edge of the royal parks, he saw the poor, the sick and the aged. Then he saw a religious beggar who seemed serene, and he realised the path his life must take.

Abandoning his riches, Siddhartha went off into the kingdoms of the Ganga Valley. For six years he begged for his food, learned to meditate, and practised severe self-mortification, but still felt no nearer to understanding life's suffering. Then, aged 35, sitting under a tree at the place now known as Bodh Gaya (south of Patna), he vowed to stay there until his goal was achieved. For 49 days he resisted the demon Mara, and became truly Enlightened; 'the Buddha' as he is called today. He preached his new wisdom at Sarnath (near Varanasi) and gathered ever more disciples. The Buddha himself converted many people. In Kushinagar, between Bodh Gaya and his birthplace, he died at the age of 80 of dysentery, it is said, from eating pork.

Preaching that suffering came from the pursuit of personal desire, the Buddha had advocated the Middle Way of the Eightfold Path: right views, right resolve, right speech, right conduct, right livelihood, right effort, right

The 'Ancient Indian' sculptural schools represented Buddha in the form of a symbol, such as a lotus, a tree, a wheel or a stupa. It was only with the emergence of the Mahayana school, patronised by the Kushan King Kanishka *(see page 28)*, that he came to be depicted in human form.

recollection and right meditation. Only thus could the enlightenment of Nirvana be achieved. This original doctrine, without any sense of the Buddha's divinity, was embraced by the Hinayana (Lesser Vehicle) school which spread to Sri Lanka, Burma, Thailand, Cambodia and Laos. The Mahayana (Great Vehicle) school added the concept of the Bodhisattva (Buddhist saint) as divine saviour, and was then the most dominant form of Buddhism, spreading to China and Japan. Vajrayana (Thunderbolt) Buddhism has much in common with Hindu Tantricism, and is particularly influential in Nepal and Tibet.

After centuries of almost total eclipse, Buddhism today has been able to achieve a revival in India, in part by offering its egalitarian philosophy to Hindu Dalits, led by B.R. Ambedkar, a campaigner for Dalit rights, as an escape from discrimination.

Jain temples in Jaisalmer

Jainism

As old as Buddhism, **Jainism** has made its mark with its concept of *ahimsa* (non-violence) and is much more pacifist than its name, which means 'religion of the conquerors'.

Vardhamana Mahavira was its founder. He was born in 599BC in Bihar and, like Buddha, was the son of a chief. He, too, abandoned riches to become an ascetic. But Mahavira (the Great Hero) pursued self-mortification to the end of his life, stripping off his clothes to take his word from kingdom to kingdom. He died of self-inflicted starvation at the age of 72 in Para, near

Rajgir. His followers were later to divide into the *Digambaras* ('sky-clad', i.e., naked) and the *Svetambaras* ('white-clad') you see today.

> **Jainism had considerable influence on Mahatma Gandhi's concept of non-violent direct action; he used its fasting-unto-death as a potent moral and political weapon.**

The religion, in which Mahavira is seen as the manifestation of 24 *Tirthankaras* (teachers, literally 'crossing makers'), attributes souls to all living creatures, as well as other natural objects. Agriculture was therefore abandoned for its destruction of plant and animal life. The doctrines survive in vegetarianism, with Jain monks and nuns carrying dusters to sweep insects away from where they tread and wearing a gauze veil over their mouth to avoid breathing in flies.

In common with Hinduism and Buddhism, Jains believe in the concepts of *karma* and rebirth. Their aim is to pass through 14 stages of the purification of the soul to gain liberation. This is achieved through right faith, right knowledge and right conduct.

Jainism claims 2 million followers in India, including many businessmen in Gujarat and the Deccan, with a few in Bengal. The Jains' non-violent religion excludes them from agriculture as a profession, but they dominate the electronics industry in Bangalore, banking in Maharashta and the diamond trade in Gujarat.

Parsis, Jews and Christians

Parsis brought Zoroastrianism from Iran in the 8th century AD, and today form only a minute community in the world of religions, with barely 100,000 living in India, mostly in and around the city of Mumbai. They have been and are still enormously influential in this country's economic life, and sometimes serve as go-betweens in the often difficult relations between Hindus and Muslims, and between India and Pakistan.

Their religion dates as far back as the 7th century BC, when their prophet Zarathustra contrasted his peaceful and sedentary People of Righteousness with the polytheistic nomadic People of Evil. Belief in the *Ahura Mazda*, the Wise Lord, is manifest

The Parsis' traditional method of corpse disposal on their Towers of Silence is under serious threat. Recent years have seen a drastic reduction in vulture numbers, thought to have been caused by the use of an anti-inflammatory drug in cattle. Vultures also keep the countryside clean by their scavenging of carrion, and their dwindling numbers have plunged this service into crisis as well – not just in Mumbai but throughout the subcontinent.

in the three principles of good thoughts, good words and good deeds.

The Parsis base their code of ethics on the concept of a constant struggle existing between the forces of creation – light and good – and those of darkness and evil. Its teachings put great emphasis on the purity of the world's natural elements: fire, earth and water. Fire plays an important part in Parsi rituals. Their places of worship are known as 'fire temples' and contain a sacred fire, which is never allowed to go out. In order to maintain the purity of the elements, Parsis do not traditionally bury or cremate their dead, but lay them exposed and naked on Towers of Silence (*Dakhma*) for the vultures to devour.

India's **Jewish** community is ancient indeed. Some texts claim that the first Jews arrived in India at the time of the Babylonian exile, in 587BC; others bring them to Cranganur, on the Malabar coast, in AD72, about the time that the disciple Thomas is said to have brought his Christian mission to India. The oldest Jewish community still in existence is situated down the coast at Kochi (Cochin), dating back at least to the 4th century AD. Some others, less orthodox, can be found in Mumbai, but most emigrated to Israel when it was founded in 1948.

The earliest **Christians** other than St Thomas, were the so-called Nestorian 'heretics' of the Syrian Orthodox Church, also living on the Malabar coast since the first centuries of the Christian era. Modern Indian Christians, some descended from the Syrians, others from those converted by British and Portuguese missionaries, number just over 24 million.

A BRIEF HISTORY

India has always been a melange of peoples. Apart from some pre-Ice Age hominids, the first settlers to arrive in India were Negritos and Proto-Australoids. Migrants of Mediterranean stock from the Middle East and Asia seem to have made up the Dravidians, now principally in the southern peninsula.

In 7000BC agriculturalists made their first appearance up in the hills of Balochistan in the northwest. In the Indus River valley, improved techniques permitted the storage of wheat and barley beyond daily needs, and from around 3000BC a well-organised society built cities at Harappa, Moenjo Daro and around 400 other sites, creating what is now known as the Indus Valley or 'Harappan' Civilisation.

Harappan cities were built mostly of solid brick

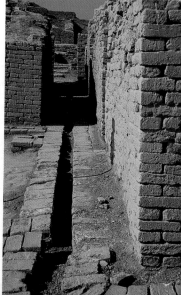

Harappan craftsmen used bricks of a standard size to build two- or three-storey houses which had sophisticated sewage and water-supply systems. Houses stood in blocks on a grid layout defined by intersecting streets. Efficient agriculture underlay this urban way of life; among the Harappan animals was a major Indian contribution to the world's food, the chicken.

Modern archaeology suggests that this civilisation was destroyed by floods, when the Indus River changed course, perhaps due to earthquakes, in about 1700BC.

The Hindus' Ancestors

The Aryans arrived on the scene some 200 years later. Originally from the steppes of Central Asia, they migrated to Mesopotamia and then on to Iran before entering India. These fair-skinned cattle-breeders, who saw the cow as an especially sacred animal, practised agriculture in the Punjab after waging war against the Dasas.

Early events surrounding the Indo-Aryans can be deduced from the later writings of the *Rigveda* (priestly hymns), *Puranas* (ancient tales of kings and gods) and the epic poems of the *Mahabharata* and *Ramayana*. These provided the basis for Hinduism; also, the epics' heroic battles suggest there was a prolonged struggle for land rights over the fertile plains north and east of modern Delhi, followed by invasions and wars.

If ancient writings give only a romanticised view, they do offer a more precise picture of Indo-Aryan society. Their long wars against the indigenous people established their leaders as

Indian miniature of a scene from the *Ramayana*

kings with a hereditary divinity, which the Brahmins (the priests) exchanged for a privileged position of their own. The caste system was already taking shape. Before the conquests, the Aryans were organised in three classes: warriors, priests and commoners. Then they established four distinct categories known as *varna* (literally, 'colour').

As possessors of magical power associated with ritual sacrifice and sacred utterance, Brahmins were the sole interpreters of the Vedic scriptures. They laid down a social pecking order with themselves in first place, followed by Kshatriyas (the warriors), Vaishyas (traders) and Shudras (agriculturalists). This organisation became more elaborate as the division of labour became more complicated, so the growing number of occupational groups were subsequently defined as *jati* (subcastes), often living in separate villages. Each caste would preserve its 'purity' by avoiding intermarriage and not sharing food with other castes. Outside these were the casteless, those of aboriginal descent, who performed the most menial tasks.

By 600BC, the Indo-Aryans had formed monarchies in the Ganga plain, surrounded by smaller tribes resisting the Brahmanic orthodoxy and its authoritarianism. Within the monarchies, thinkers took to the asceticism that has characterised spiritual life in India. The Brahmins cannily countered this threat by absorbing the new ideas into their teachings. But the tribes were less amenable and so became the breeding ground for two new religions espousing non-violence: Jainism and Buddhism.

While rulers fought for control of the Ganga Valley, new invaders appeared at India's frontiers; Cyrus, emperor of Persia, crossed the Hindu Kush mountains into the Indus Valley in 530BC. While Brahmin and Persian scholars exchanged ideas, the Indians copied the Persian coin system. Rock inscriptions left by Emperor Darius probably inspired the pillar-edicts of Indian Emperor Asoka in the 3rd century BC.

The spectacular invasion by Alexander the Great of Macedonia in 326BC ended Persian presence, but apart from opening up trade with Asia Minor and the eastern Mediterranean, the

Greeks had no lasting impact on India during the two-year campaign. Alexander's dreams of a huge empire extending eastwards across the Ganga plain were blocked by mutinous troops fed up with upset stomachs, the harsh terrain and the tough Indian military opposition. He returned to Babylon, leaving a few governors on the frontier.

The Mauryan Empire

Meanwhile, in the Ganga Valley power struggle, Magadha (modern Bihar) emerged as the dominant kingdom. Its ruler, Chandragupta Maurya (321–297BC), was also to become the founder of India's first imperial dynasty with Pataliputra (modern Patna), the world's largest city at the time, as its capital.

The *Didarganj Yakshi*, a famous Mauryan statue from Patna

Chandragupta extended his rule to the northwest with a rigorous campaign against the forces of Seleucus Nikator, one of Alexander's generals who had founded the Seleucid dynasty in Iran. It ended in a marriage alliance with the Greeks, but later Chandragupta turned to more sober thoughts: he converted to Jainism, and finally starved to death at the temple of Sravanabelagola.

His son Bindusara combined his father's ambition with a taste for the good life and philosophy. He expanded the empire as far down as Mysore and stunned the Western world by asking the Seleucid King Antiochus for Greek wine, figs and a sophist. The king was happy to send the wine and figs, but would not, however, consent to Bindusara's last request.

To control land and sea routes to the south, the Mauryas still needed to conquer the eastern kingdom of Kalinga (modern Orissa). The task was left to Bindusara's heir Asoka (269–232BC), admired by Indians as their greatest ruler, perhaps for his special combination of tough authoritarianism and a high sense of moral righteousness. Asoka began by killing all his rivals before conquering Kalinga in 260BC. This left 100,000 dead, with even more dying from famine and disease, while 150,000 were taken captive.

Asoka holds a special place within the modern state as his lion-topped pillar is the emblem of the Government of India. Recently he was transformed into a heart-throb through the big-budget blockbuster movie, *Asoka*, starring Shah Rukh Khan and Kareena Kapoor.

Famous inscriptions on rocks and pillars everywhere bore testimony to Asoka's reign. The inscriptions state how 'he of gentle visage and beloved of the gods', as he described himself, was filled with remorse and converted to the non-violent teachings of Buddha. But metaphysical implications seem to have interested him less than enforcing a moral example to unite his far-flung subjects in peace and fellowship, under him. To oversee this mass conversion, Asoka turned the Brahmanic concept of *dharma* (righteousness) into an instrument of public policy, enforced by the Officers of Righteousness he had appointed for this purpose. The imperial administration for this undertaking demanded a huge bureaucracy, with superintendents, accountants and clerks overseeing commerce, forestry, armory, weights and measures, goldsmiths, prostitutes, ships, cows and horses, elephants, chariots and infantry. Southern India remained independent, but Asoka had his hands full with a large empire that now extended as far north as Kashmir and east to Bengal.

In the 50 years that followed Asoka's death, Mauryan power went into decline. Agriculture was not productive enough to

Buddhist caves at Ajanta

finance the empire's expansion. Also, the unwieldy bureaucracy could not keep its loyalties straight, with the too-rapid turnover in rulers vying for Asoka's throne.

Kushan Rule

After the break-up of the Mauryan empire, new invaders appeared on the northwest frontier. The first to arrive were Bactrian Greeks left in the Afghan hills by Alexander's successors. They were welcomed for their erudite ideas on medicine, astronomy and astrology.

Joined by Iranian kings known as Pahlavas, the Greeks were overrun in the 1st century BC by bands of Scythian nomads known as the Shakas. They moved on into the Ganga valley when other nomads, the Yueh-chi from Central Asia, swept across the frontier.

Emerging victorious from the struggles between the Yueh-chi and the Shakas, King Kanishka of the Kushan branch of the Yueh-chi established an empire extending from the northern half of India into Central Asia. This put the Kushans in control of the east–west trade that plied the Silk Road between Rome and Xian in China. It was a position from which they derived enormous wealth, and under Kanishka this was ploughed into the development of art and culture. Kanishka was a champion of the Mahayana (Great Vehicle) school of Buddhism, which attributed for the first time a quasi-divinity to Buddha; his active patronage of the arts led to the creation of the first bronze and stone sculptures of Buddha – the Buddha in human form.

Buddhist and Jain merchants prospered from the new Silk Road trade and so were able to finance the magnificently sculpted cave-temples in the Deccan, including those at Ajanta and Ellora; in the northwest, the region of Gandhara (around Peshawar in present-day Pakistan) was transformed into a major monastic centre from which the message of Buddhism was sent out to the world. The arts also flourished in southern India during these early times. Madurai was the lively cultural centre for Dravidian artists: poets, actors, singers, musicians, and also dancers who were the precursors of the Hindu *devadasi* temple dancers.

Gupta Glory

The Gupta dynasty, founded by the obscure Bihari landowner Chandra Gupta I, rose to power during the 4th century AD. Marriage alliance and military conquest allowed the Guptas to create an empire stretching from Bengal to the Punjab and from Kashmir to the Deccan.

Samudra Gupta, the warrior of the clan, launched lightning raids through the jungles to snatch the gold of the south. The Guptas also captured the western seaports and their trade with the Arabs. They turned their noses up at trade with the Romans, but China offered many bounties, such as silk, musk and amber, in exchange for India's spices, jewels and perfumes, as well as colourful parakeets for the ladies' boudoirs and monkeys for their cooking pots.

The Gupta empire began to crumble in the 5th century, with the onslaught of the so-called White Huns. They were not clearly linked to Attila's Huns, but their harsh agenda of exterminating

Buddhists does suggest an affinity. The White Huns seized the Punjab, Kashmir and a large portion of the western Ganga plain before being chased out again.

In the 7th century, one strong king, Harshavardhana, reigned for 40 years over northern India, and encouraged Buddhist monks and Brahmin priests to participate in philosophical discussions. Sages developed the strict disciplines of yoga and profound metaphysical speculations of Vedanta.

In southern India, power was shared by the Pallavas in Kanchipuram and the Pandyas and Cholas vying for control of Thanjavur (Tanjore) and the fertile Kaveri Delta. The *bhakti* movement of the Tamils brought a new warmth to the hitherto rigid Brahmanic ritual of Hinduism. The temples of Mamallapuram were a high point in southern architecture, and it was the Pallavan artists who influenced – and may have helped to build – the temples at Angkor Wat in Cambodia and Borobudur in Java.

Bhakti

The *bhakti* movement arose during the 4th to 6th centuries AD in southern India as a response to both Brahmanical Hinduism rooted in the Vedas and the stringent rules of Jainism and Buddhism. Moving away from ritual presided over by temple priests and positing a personal relationship with the divine as the central religious experience, it proved immensely popular and became the driving force in the wholesale revival of Hinduism in South Asia after a long period of Buddhist dominance. Spread in part though the teachings of wandering singer-saints, its influence has remained intense up to the present-day, with the songs of *bhaktas* such as Mirabai and Tyagaraja continuing to be performed; particularly important is the story of Krishna and Radha who become the divine lovers to whom the devotee bares his or her soul. This powerful devotional tradition found its Islamic counterpart in the Sufis who arrived in around the 10th century AD *(see page 33)* and the creative tension and blurring of the two traditions formed a uniquely tolerant Indo-Islamic culture.

Islam Comes to India

Arab trade with India had long since whetted the appetites of the Muslims; when Indian pirates plundered their ships off the coast of Sindh in 711, it provoked the governor of Chaldea (now Iraq) to send troops with 6,000 horses and 6,000 camels to conquer the Sindh rajas and offer the alternative of converting to Islam or death. When it was revealed to the governor of Chaldea that Hinduism was in fact a serious religion with too many faithful to treat in this way, another solution had to be found: Hindus, along with Parsis who had fled an earlier Muslim persecution in Persia, were given the privileged status of *dhimmi*, dues-paying non-believers.

Jama Masjid (Friday Mosque) in Delhi

For nearly 300 years, Islamic conquest in India was confined to this trading community in Sindh, but in the 10th century, tribesmen from Turkistan, driven west by Chinese expansion, set up a state at Ghazni and began raids across the border to plunder Hindu temples. Sweeping through the Punjab and Gujarat across to the western end of the Ganga valley, Mahmud of Ghazni (997–1030) used these raids more to finance his empire in Persia and Turkistan than to set up a permanent foothold in India. Mahmud smashed the infidels' idols and destroyed their temples as he went, but was nonetheless cultured enough to use the booty to build a library, a museum and a splendid mosque when he got back to Ghazni. If Muslims saw him as a righteous militant and Hindus as a brutal monster, neither denied him his title of 'Sword of Islam'. In order to understand his ambiguous image, compare him with Europe's heroic crusaders who went on the rampage at about the same time.

Sculpted frieze at Khajuraho

There was no concerted Indian response to the invasions because the various kingdoms were busy with wars of their own. The Rajput warrior clans fought each other for control in what is now Rajasthan, the Kathiawar peninsula, and as far east as Khajuraho. The Turco-Afghan invaders were regarded as a transient phenomenon that would either soon disappear or, just like others before them, be swallowed up by the great subcontinent.

A Sultan for Delhi

At the end of the 12th century, the Turks arrived: Sultan Mohammed of Ghur and his Mameluke (slave) General Qutb-ud-din Aybak seized Ghazni in 1173 and invaded India. The Rajputs made a belated alliance and fought valiantly from one desert fortress to another, but their elephants could not match their opponents' fast horses and Afghan cavalry firing superior crossbows at the gallop. By 1193, the Turks were masters in Peshawar, Lahore and Delhi. The sultan returned to Ghazni and, leaving Qutb-ud-din in charge, moved east to Bengal, destroying centres of Buddhism such as the University of Nalanda.

After his master's assassination in 1206, Qutb-ud-din proclaimed himself sultan of Delhi, head of India's first Islamic dynasty. The sultanate lasted 320 years, but the new sultan ruled for only four years as he died in a fall from his pony.

After the shock of the invasion had passed, the Turks proved to be a shot in the arm for India. The Persian language spoken at court enriched Indian literature and combined with the Sanskrit-based dialects of northern India to create Hindustani. Painting and architecture were infused with life, roads were paved, and, in the 14th century, Delhi was pronounced by the Arab traveller Ibn Batuta to be the most magnificent city in the whole Muslim world. Conversion to the Islamic faith was seen as a means of advancement, and those Rajputs who didn't take advantage of this offer were able to sharpen their martial skills in constant guerrilla warfare. The Turks adopted the Indian cuisine and costume as well as a modified form of the Hindu caste system. Highest were those of foreign extraction such as Turks, Arabs, Afghans and Persians, known as *ashraf* (that is, 'honourable'). Then came upper-caste converts from Hinduism, the 'clean' castes of both merchants and artisans, and then the 'unclean' occupations of scavengers.

It is worth noting that the first – and last – Muslim woman to rule in India was Qutb-ud-din's granddaughter Raziyya. 'Wise, just, and generous', noted a contemporary Muslim historian, 'but she was not born of the right sex and so all the virtues were worthless'.

Decades before Islam was imposed on northern India by the swords of invaders, a benign and inclusive form of the faith was introduced by wandering missionary-mystics, known as the Sufis, who renounced materialism and sought to draw close to God through direct spiritual experience. The Sufi legacy continues to be felt in India today, particularly at the shrines of its major saints, where devotional, ecstatic *Qawwali* music is performed each Friday evening.

Three years of her wisdom, justice and generosity were all her political dynasty's opponents could take before she was murdered.

Next came Ala-ud-din Khalji (1296–1316), who forced Mongol invaders back across the Afghan frontier and then moved through the peninsula to its southern tip. But Ala-ud-din's successors, the Tughlaq dynasty, did not assert control of the territory. The south remained dominated by the Hindu kingdom of Vijayanagar for the next 250 years.

The Delhi sultanate under the Tughlaq dynasty could no longer hold its own in the north, and so Muslim kingdoms began to form in Bengal and the Deccan. The end was hastened by the Mongol Timur the Lame. Perceiving that the sultans were a soft target, he cut through Delhi in 1398, slaughtering thousands of Hindus and carrying off thousands more as slaves. He left behind him famine and pestilence. The Turks' Indian empire in splinters, it passed into the hands of the Afghan Lodis, who later succumbed to Timur's descendants, the Mughals.

Down on the Malabar coast, the great Portuguese explorer Vasco da Gama landed in 1498, paving the way for his countrymen to form a settlement further north in Goa a decade or so later. The merchants wanted to divert trade away from the Arabs, fearing the enrichment of the North African Maghreb as a threat to Christian Europe. They first tried offering cloth, wine and necklaces for ivory and gold, but the traders of Calicut were insulted at being taken for fools who could be bought with cheap hooch and glass baubles. The Portuguese turned instead to the harder sell of naval batteries, driving off a trading fleet in the year 1509 in order to control the coast.

With the Portuguese merchant adventurers came Jesuit missionaries, who found the best subjects for their teachings among the low-caste Hindus. Around 1548 Francis Xavier began his mission among the pearl fishermen of the Malabar, before he set sail for Japan. To deal with the small communities of Jews and Nestorian Christian 'heretics', who had settled down on the Malabar coast in the mists of antiquity, the then archbishop of Goa opened a local branch of the dreaded Holy Inquisition.

The Great Mughals

The new conquerors of northern India did not come uninvited. The Afghan governors of the Sindh and the Punjab, who were hoping for more autonomy than they had under Sultan Ibrahim Lodi in Delhi, therefore called on Babur the Tiger, king of Kabul.

Babur, descendant of Timur the Lame and of Genghis Khan, accepted their welcome but made no promises. His men crushed Sultan Ibrahim's 50,000-strong army with matchlocks and mortars, hitherto unknown in India, at Panipat, north of Delhi.

It was the morning of 21 April 1526, the beginning of

Babur in his garden

the empire of the Mughals – the term used for descendants of Babur as distinct from those of Genghis Khan, who are referred to as 'Mongols' even though the terms are etymologically the same. Babur fought resistance from the Rajputs and captured Delhi and Agra, then conquered the Afghan chiefs in 1529. His empire stretched from the Oxus River (Amu Darya) in the west to Bengal in the east, with a southern limit marked by the Rajasthan Desert.

Babur died in 1530. His heir, Humayun, preferred opium and astrology to complex state affairs; he was driven out of India into Persia by General Sher Shah, who proved to be a much more able ruler. In five years, the general built new roads, created a royal postal service, and set the pattern of Mughal administration that would endure for the next two centuries before dying in battle and leaving the throne to a number of inept successors and, eventually, the return of Humayun.

Humayun came back in 1555 with a Persian army to recapture the Punjab, Delhi and Agra, but the next year his opium habit caused his death *(see page 68)*.

His son, Jalal-ud-din Mohammed Akbar (1556–1605), was a very able ruler. Typical of his genius was the new religion he offered his subjects: the Divine Faith (Din-Ilahi), intended to satisfy orthodox Muslims and those who, like himself and the Hindus, appreciated the idea of a semi-divine ruler. Keen to win the allegiance of the Hindus, Akbar abolished most of the discriminatory taxes on non-Muslims, and recruited Rajputs for his army after marrying a daughter of Raja Bharmal of Amber (though he did not flinch at massacring another 8,000 Rajput soldiers).

But despite repeated efforts, Akbar could not extend his empire south. In 1565, the Muslim sultanates of the Deccan had taken the Hindu empire of Vijayanagar by means of slaughter, but they were not going to hand it all to Akbar.

Harems: the Cold Facts

The Indian Muslims' system of purdah, which strictly confined women to a life behind a screen in special apartments, derived from the old Persian institution of the harem. No men were allowed in the vicinity and armed security guards inside were all female, except for eunuchs who were placed at the outside doors.

In Akbar's time, women were admitted to the harem as an honour to their families, an imperial favour to some politically useful noble, certainly not always nor even very often for the emperor's sexual pleasure. Though he might have had several hundred wives, very few were his regular companions.

The senior wife, mistress of the household, was a person of great influence in the realm, guardian of one of the two imperial seals needed to authorise a new statute, and the emperor's confidante in many of his decisions. The most famous example was Mumtaz, wife of Shah Jahan, but Jahangir's wife, Nur Jahan, was much more powerful; she practically ran the whole country.

Humayun's tomb in Delhi

Although illiterate, Akbar demonstrated enormous intellectual curiosity. He preferred sufi mysticism to orthodox Islam, and held debates with Brahmins, Jain monks, Zoroastrians and Jesuits. The more orthodox Muslims were concerned that Islam was being abandoned, and rebellions sprang up in Bengal, Bihar and the Punjab.

While Akbar was fighting in the Deccan in 1601, his son claimed the throne. Akbar rushed back to reassert his power but he died soon after, poisoned, it is rumoured, by his son. The new emperor called himself Jahangir (World Seizer) but once in power he left affairs of state to his wife, Nur Jahan, and her father, Mirza Ghiyath Beg, as he was more interested in writing poetry, drinking a great deal of wine, and taking summer excursions up to Kashmir. Here, rich Persian culture dictated taste in dress, décor, manners and morals, enriched by the Hindu culture of the Rajputs in literature, cuisine and sexuality. If the peasants were squeezed by taxes to pay for the luxury of Mughal court life, it was a boon for the country's artisans: goldsmiths, jewellers and weavers. In such an atmosphere, incidents of highway banditry increased and the district governors shared the rich booty in exchange for a pardon when the bandits were captured.

Jahangir's son Shah Jahan became the biggest spender of all the Mughals. He lavished millions on palaces and mosques, shelling out at least one million pounds sterling on gold and jewels for his Peacock Throne. Despite this, the imperial treasury allotted only 5,000 rupees a week for the plague and famine victims of 1631. Of several hundred women in the emperor's harem, his only love was the now legendary Mumtaz-Mahal ('Exalted of the Palace'), by whom he had 14 children in a period of 17 years. When she died, Shah Jahan built her the most famous memorial a man ever offered to the woman he loved: the Taj Mahal.

Shah Jahan's son was Aurangzeb (1658–1707), who overthrew his father and imprisoned him in the Agra fort for the last years of his life. A pious Muslim, puritanical in both clothes and personal tastes, he banished music from the court and burned the portraits of princes as breaches of the Islamic taboo on graven images. Gone, too, was any notion of religious tolerance. The Sikhs were slaughtered, the Hindu temples in both Varanasi and Mathura were destroyed, and the building of new temples was forbidden. Taxes on non-Muslims were brought back; Hindu merchants were forced to pay double duties on their goods. Aurangzeb streamlined the lax administration of his predecessors, but he almost

Shah Jahan on his throne

bankrupted the realm with his campaigns to expand the empire down to the south, and his battles against rebels in the north. The most significant resistance came from Marathas, in today's State of Maharashtra, around Bombay. They were led by the fighter Shivaji (1627–1680), bandit, brave military commander and an authentic Hindu folk hero.

Starting out from Pune, Shivaji's Marathas fought off the Deccan sultans at Bijapur and the Mughals at Purandar. Aurangzeb forced him finally to submit, but the humiliating reception he was given at court sent him back on the warpath again. Shivaji then had himself crowned king of the Marathas and, to pay his soldiers, plundered the country all the way east to Madras.

> **The Mughal style of miniature painting came out of a fusion of Persian and native art. Initiated by Humayun, the style flourished under Akbar, who left a library of some 24,000 manuscripts, and his son, Jahangir, known for his delight in representations of the natural world. Shah Jahan continued the tradition, but later the artists went to regional courts and painting at the Moghul court declined.**

The British Arrive

Meanwhile, by the middle of the 17th century, Dutch and British armed merchant ships had broken through the Portuguese blockade to set up their East India companies on both coasts. Arriving in 1608, the British took five years to get their foot in the Indian door, at the western port of Surat, north of Bombay. The British East India Company destroyed the Portuguese fleet and took over the protection of the Muslim pilgrimage ships to Mecca, but that didn't stop the Portuguese making a gift of Bombay (then a tiny, swamp-ridden trading post) to King Charles II in 1661 as part of the dowry of Catherine of Braganza. The Indians were not consulted.

The Company erected its east-coast installations, or 'factories', in the year 1642 just down the road from the Dutch, at Mandaraz,

Robert Clive

pronounced 'Madras' by the British. Further north, the British gradually gained the upper hand over their rivals, now including the French, for the Bengali trade that was to create Calcutta.

The Mughal empire had five rulers in 12 years after Aurangzeb died. Bihar, Bengal and Rajputana all went their separate ways. The Sikhs reacted violently to persecution, and the Marathas spread to Orissa, after which, in the year 1739, Nadir Shah of Persia invaded and carried off the Mughal Peacock Throne (broken up after his assassination). Meanwhile, the British clerk-turned-soldier Robert Clive won a long campaign against the French for possession of Madras.

Fearing the Europeans would start carving up Bengal, the *nawab* (Muslim prince) Siraj-ud-daula set up an attack on the British settlement in Calcutta on the hot day of 20 June 1756. Those who did not flee to sea were thrown into Fort William's prison, already known as the Black Hole. It is still being debated whether 123 suffocated and 23 survived or 'only' 43 died, leaving 21 survivors, but however many did perish provided provocation enough for Clive to crush Siraj-ud-daula at the Battle of Plassey. Clive became governor and placed his own nawab on the throne, in exchange for £500,000 for himself and the East India Company. He then annexed about 2,330 sq km (900 sq miles) of land due south of Calcutta to provide rents for the British settlement and to guarantee himself an income of £30,000 per year for life. The rise of the British empire in India had begun.

Installing the Raj

The arrival of Indian merchants, including Jains, Parsis and Jews, turned Bombay, Madras and Calcutta into large cities; while the East India Company discovered a knack for large-scale administration. A more ordered form of exploitation took the place of what Clive called 'fighting, chicanery, intrigues, politics, and Lord knows what'. In return for fixed payments to the emperor, Company officials collected revenue. With a well-paid civil service, Clive's successors – Warren Hastings and Lord Cornwallis – avoided the collectors by padding their salaries with private deals. With the title of governor-general, the new 'viceroys' were responsible to the British government rather than the East India Company. Britain began taking India more seriously. But this new interest had in it the seeds of future discontent. Indians were removed from key positions in the administration by Cornwallis, and it took a long time for them to be readmitted to positions of responsibility.

Clive's example in Calcutta set the pattern for territorial control around the country. In the south, Tipu Sultan of Mysore remained a menace to Madras until Governor-General Arthur Wellesley, the future Duke of Wellington, defeated him. Wellesley then turned on the Marathas, whose clans controlled the puppet Mughal emperor in Delhi and much of central India. A few brilliant victories gained control of Orissa and other territories for Britain, but London decided all that energy would be best directed at Napoleon, and called Wellesley home.

When territory wasn't acquired by conquest – Sindh from Baloch princes, Punjab and Kashmir from the Sikhs, Maharashtra and Delhi from the Marathas, or Assam from Burma – the British annexed it by so-called Principles of Lapse and Paramountcy. If a ruler died without direct heir, his state 'lapsed' into British hands. If, after repeated warnings, a state was judged guilty of misgovernment, it was simply annexed by the Paramount Power – the British.

Schools and colleges were established. Calcutta became the centre of a vigorous free press and the intellectual capital of India. During 1834, regional rupees of differing value were minted with the portrait of the Mughal emperor. Then a national rupee of unitary value was issued, with the face of the king of England. In the interests of running the empire effectively, the British installed railways, better roads, the telegraph and

A Short History of Kashmir

This mainly mountainous region entered the history books in the 3rd century BC when Emperor Asoka is said to have sent Buddhist missionaries to found the town of Srinagar. Kashmir became a centre of Hindu culture in medieval times, but its Hindu kings were defeated by Afghans in the 14th century. With their equal enthusiasm for both iconoclasm and creativity, the Muslim invaders smashed the Hindu temples and introduced the arts of silk weaving, shawl embroidery, wood carving and ornamental papier mâché that have been the glory of Kashmir ever since.

Kashmir flourished under the Mughals, who annexed it in 1585, Akbar appreciating the sweet fruits of its orchards that he missed in the plains, and Jahangir and Shah Jahan laying out gardens that provoked the envy of Louis XIV when he heard about them. With the decline of the Mughal empire in the 18th century, Kashmir faced successive invasions, first by the Persian Nadir Shah, then, in the 1750s, by the Afghan Ahmad Shah Durrani. In 1819, the Sikhs led by the Punjab's powerful ruler Ranjit Singh, pushed the Afghans back to the Khyber Pass.

Then came the British. In 1846, they took the state away from the Sikhs and handed it to Gulab Singh, a Hindu Rajput prince, under British protection, even though Muslims formed (as they still do) an overwhelming majority of the population. Gulab Singh's descendants continued to rule in Kashmir right up to the abolition of the princes in 1952. Muslim invaders tried to overthrow the incumbent Hari Singh at Partition in 1947; he was rescued by the Indian Army only on condition that he agreed to Kashmir's joining India rather than Pakistan. Three wars have been fought over Kashmir since then, and violence and accusations continue.

stamp-post. Indians also saw the other side of the Industrial Revolution as their cotton left for Manchester to come back as cloth cheaper than their own. Men such as Governor-General William Bentinck worked with missionaries and reformers such as Brahmin Ram Mohan Roy to legislate against the practice of widows becoming sati by climbing onto the funeral pyres of their husbands. Other campaigns were launched against female infanticide, slavery and the bands of *Thugs* (devotees of Kali) ranging the countryside.

Some rajas became British vassals

Although some Indians assimilated the language and behaviour of the British, to most the imperialists were offensively aloof. The Indians had known other conquerors, but at least they had been able to gain a sense of them as human beings. The British Raj, though, was firmly entrenched in clubs, and remained resolutely separate.

Rebellion and Reform

The cause of the Uprising of 1857, or the First War of Independence as it is known to Indians, was symptomatic of British insensitivity. Indian troops were trained to bite the cartridges before loading their rifles, but some were greased with animal fat and the Indians felt they were ingesting either fat from the cow, sacred to the Hindus, or lard from the pig, abomination to the Muslims. As they had suffered slights of either incomprehension or contempt for their religious customs before, they simply could not believe it was not deliberate, and an insurrection broke out at Meerut, 40km (25 miles) north of Delhi.

Fierce fighting around Lucknow dring the Mutiny of 1857

The cartridge blunder became a pretext for avenging other grievances, with troops rallying around the rulers dispossessed by Lapse or Paramountcy. The rebellious army sepoys then invaded Delhi, Kanpur (Cawnpore) and Lucknow, looting treasuries, breaking open jails, and killing British men, women and children.

The British retaliated with equal savagery against the rebels and against civilians in the country through which the relief columns passed. Finally, after re-taking the hub of the rebellion, Delhi, they condemned the last of the proud Mughals, Emperor Bahadur Shah, to exile in Burma. Nothing could more aptly epitomise the Mutiny's good and bad results, from an Indian point of view, than the name given to the legislation that was to follow: the 1858 Act for Better Government of India. The British decided to tighten their imperial hold.

The East India Company was replaced by a government with a viceroy answering to a secretary of state for India in London. The bureaucracy was to be streamlined, and the army reorganised to raise the ratio of British to Indians. Indian education was greatly expanded, though less successfully in rural areas where people thought it better to be a good peasant than a bad clerk. Queen Victoria, who in the year 1876 would add the title empress of India to her roll of honour, proclaimed that the Indian Civil Service would be open to 'our subjects of whatever race and creed'. However, not a lot of Indians could afford the trip to Britain to take the examination.

Meanwhile, lawyers were at a premium – litigation had become something of a passion in India and it was ideal training for future politicians – and open political debate flourished, especially in Calcutta where Karl Marx was much appreciated (politics had been clandestine up to now because it was so often fatal to express an opinion on the wrong – that is, losing – side).

Modern industry came to the subcontinent, with Indian entrepreneurs developing their own cotton mills in Bombay, Ahmadabad, Kanpur and Madras. But the new tea plantations were a strictly British affair. Indian agricultural products soon found new markets in Europe when the Suez Canal was opened in 1869.

British economic policies were having a devastating impact on the rural peasants. A series of protracted, severe droughts between 1876 and 1902 sparked off food shortages that were compounded by the viceroys' refusal to cap grain prices. As huge quantities of surplus wheat were exported to England, prices soared and poor farmers died in droves. It is now estimated that between 12 and 40 million Indians perished in the ensuing famines.

In the arts, architecture was often the work of engineers, and huge sculptures were ordered from Victorian Britain rather than from local artists. The bright spot was the Archaeological Survey of

Queen Victoria, Empress of India

1871 to preserve ancient monuments. British soldiers hunting tigers in the jungle were finding temples and palaces many Indians no longer knew existed.

Fighting for Self-Rule

The Indian National Congress, the country's first political party, held its inaugural meeting in Bombay in 1885. As a group of liberal Hindu and Parsi intellectuals, supported by a few progressive British, it was more national in purpose than in its representation. Lacking connection with the peasants, it was also distrusted by conservative landlords and by most Muslims. The goal of *swaraj* (self-rule), proclaimed in 1906, was seen by a moderate Centre group as government within the British empire, and by a breakaway revolutionary Left group as complete independence.

After years of subservience to the West, artists returned to Indian themes in their literature, theatre and music. Indians applauded the decision of Lord Ripon to allow Indian magistrates to try British defendants in criminal cases, but attempts at social reform such as protecting child brides against rape by their husbands were fought by traditionalist Hindus from Calcutta and Pune with cries of 'religion in danger'. Self-assertion reigned again: after years of peace, hostilities broke out between the Hindus and the Muslims.

After the uprisings in 1857, communal 'divide and rule' became the watchword for the British in India. For example, through the census they forced people to identify themselves in terms of their religion. This fuelled religious tensions in the subcontinent, which persist to this day.

In Maharashtra, a Hindu nationalist cult grew up around the Maratha leader Shivaji *(see page 39)* against the British and also the Muslims whom Shivaji had fought all his life. Fundamentalists took to the streets to protest against the Muslim slaughter of cows. There was a movement to convert Muslims and Christians back to the 'national' religion. Muslims tried to purify Islamic practice of the Hindu rituals which had accrued over the years.

The caste system was affected by this new spirit. The low caste and casteless pressed for better treatment, but their cause was not helped by the activism of American missionaries and the Salvation Army, who gave other castes a good excuse to resist 'foreign interference'.

Dynamic Lord Curzon, viceroy from 1899 to 1905, was driven by a lofty imperial vision of the British role in India. His grandiose life in the viceregal residence in Calcutta or palace in Simla was worthy of the Mughal emperors.

Highly active in excavating and restoring the temples and palaces, Curzon also did more than any of his predecessors, adding 9,000km (5,500 miles) of new railway lines, working to modernise farming with an agricultural research institute, and building an irrigation system that would become a model for Asia and Africa. But Curzon also tightened press censorship, restored aristocratic privileges and refused to sanction 'indiscriminate alms giving' in the face of massive famine. The Indians also resented his refusal to consult them, and rioted over an ill-considered partition of Bengal. All of this contributed to civil unrest and calls for independence.

In 1911, King George V became the first British monarch to visit India. He celebrated the fact by announcing that

Lord Curzon

the capital would be moved from Calcutta to a whole new city to be built in Delhi. The Royal architects Edwin Lutyens and Herbert Baker created a monumental New Delhi with triumphal arches, palaces, gigantic government buildings and sweeping avenues radiating from circles (for easy riot control) – the stuff of an empire meant to last forever.

In 1917 self-determination in India seemed nearer when London announced its plan for 'the progressive realization of responsible government in India as an integral part of the (British) Empire'. The British were not letting go, but a new Government of India Act two years later promised Indians real executive power at the head of provincial ministries for education, public works, health and agriculture. The moderate Indians were delighted, the revolutionaries saw it as a foot in the door, while many British officials retired rather than serve under Indian ministers.

Riots over Bengal's partition led to new laws for political trials without jury and also internment without trial. Popular protest in the big cities in 1919 at first took the non-violent form of a *hartal*, an Indian 'strike' called when the soul is shocked by an injustice. This idea came from the new leader Mohandas Karamchand Gandhi, dubbed Mahatma (Great Soul) by the Indian poet Rabindranath Tagore.

Gandhi returned to India in 1915 after working as a lawyer defending the rights of the Indian community in South Africa.

Without giving up demands for self-determination, India fought at Britain's side in World War I, and more than one German general blinked at Rajput and Sikh princes leading Indian infantry across the trenches of the Western Front.

The moral strength of his non-violent philosophy was immediately tested in the Punjab, where the *hartal* erupted into riots. In Amritsar, the troops of General Reginald Dyer fired on a prohibited mass meeting, leaving 379 dead and over 1,200 wounded.

As a result, gradualist reform became discredited and civil unrest a feature of everyday life. Declaring that 'cooperation in any form with this satanic government is sinful', Gandhi advocated the boycott of elections and the withdrawal of people from government office. Moderates held on, but the election boycott was at least 33 percent successful.

Abandoning European dress for a white cotton *dhoti* (loincloth) and shawl, and drawing spiritual guidance from all the great religions of India, Gandhi became the simple but powerful symbol of India. He supported the so-called 'untouchable' castes, whom he dubbed 'Harijans' (Children of God), and defended the rights of village artisans and peasants, but his non-violent movement could not stop the worsening riots among the religious communities.

Gandhi as a young lawyer

Worried by the spread of his civil disobedience movement, the British jailed Gandhi in 1922 for two years. In jail at the same time, for 'incitement to rebellion', was Congress Party member Jawaharlal Nehru, who was British-educated but also a Brahmin intellectual, as his honorary title of Pandit suggested. He was the Mahatma's favourite to lead India to independence.

Independence with Partition

The British began to see India's independence as inevitable; however, only a few seemed to understand the vital role of the country's religious groups. Britain prepared a parliamentary democracy with majority rule, but the majority were Hindus – and Hindus, Muslims and Sikhs had been vying for power for many centuries.

Nehru's Congress Party, largely Hindu with a socialist leadership, wanted a parliamentary democracy. As counterweight, British legislation reserved parliamentary seats for religious minorities, but the Punjab and Bengal had such a complicated mixture of Hindus, Muslims and Sikhs that it was not possible to avoid fights over how separate constituencies were to be formed.

The legislation on reserving seats gave the Muslims the basis for an alternative to an India in which they made up only a quarter of the population: Partition. In 1930, the poet Muhammad Iqbal proposed a separate Muslim homeland in the northwest of India. A small group of Indian Muslims at Cambridge came up with the name Pakistan, using the initials of the Punjab, Afghania (Northwest Frontier Province), Kashmir and Sindh (at the same time producing the word *pak*, meaning 'pure' in Urdu), and adding *stan*, the Persian suffix for the word 'country'. The Muslim campaign for Partition was led by the London-trained Bombay lawyer, Muhammad Ali Jinnah.

Statue of Gandhi leading his Salt March to the sea

Meanwhile, Gandhi vehemently opposed any dismemberment of the country, and tried to keep people united by fasting to uphold the spirit of love, and by focusing on the common adversary: the British. Advocating civil disobedience, he led his famous

Winston Churchill bitterly opposed Indian independence, and so it was probably as well for India that he was defeated by Attlee's Labour Party in the election of 1945.

Salt March to the sea, to scoop up salt and circumvent the hated British salt tax. This put more than 60,000 in jail.

Against this backdrop of militancy, World War II did not elicit the solidarity of the first. Indians courageously fought alongside British troops, in Burma, the Middle East and Europe, but Gandhi saw the British as a provocation for Japanese invasion and was jailed yet again, for launching a 'Quit India' campaign in 1942. Led by Subhash Chandra Bose (aka Netaji) some anti-British extremists even saw the Japanese as a potential Asian liberator.

With riots growing ever more bloody in Bengal, Bihar and the Punjab, India's last viceroy, Lord Mountbatten, kept a mandate to make the British departure as quick and as smooth as possible. Quick it was – six months after his arrival – but not smooth. Midnight, 14–15 August, in the year 1947, was a moment, in the words of Prime Minister Nehru, 'when we step out from the old to the new, when an age ends, and when the soul of a nation, long suppressed, finds utterance'.

Nehru got his Independence and Jinnah his Partition – a Pakistan whose eastern Bengali portion was to break away 24 years later to become Bangladesh. Bloodshed began as soon as the Partition boundaries were set. In east (Indian) Punjab, Hindus and Sikhs massacred Muslims; in west (Pakistani) Punjab, the Muslims massacred Sikhs and Hindus. This was followed by a mass exodus of millions from one country to the other, but the convoys often ended in slaughter. Delhi itself was torn apart by communal rampages. The overall death toll during Partition amounted to at least 500,000 people.

Mountbatten, Nehru and Jinnah in Independence negotiations

Mahatma Gandhi immediately rushed from Calcutta to Delhi to defend Muslims against further slaughter. In January 1948, he fasted for peace in the capital city in order to force the Indian government to pay Pakistan the monies due in the Partition's division of assets. A Hindu fanatic, enraged by what he felt was an excessively fervent defence of Muslim interests, assassinated Gandhi at a prayer meeting on 30 January.

India Today

Sensitive and sophisticated, Pandit Nehru was also the strongest ruler India had known since the great Mughals and, like them, he created a powerful dynasty. Rejecting his mentor Gandhi's faith in a village-based democracy, Nehru worked to make India a fully industrialised society on the basis of democratic social-ism. Established industries had their taxes raised but were not nationalised. Companies that were foreign had to accept Indian financial participation and management.

He appropriated for the state much of the personal fortunes of the princes, but found it harder to curtail the power of landowners who had extensive contacts with the more conservative elements in his Congress Party.

Nehru's native Kashmir remained an unresolved problem of Partition. The Muslim majority in the Vale of Kashmir and Gilgit made it part of Pakistan, but the greater part of the eastern region around Jammu was Hindu, as was the maharaja, Hari Singh. Backed by Pakistan, Pathan tribesmen invaded Kashmir in 1947 to force the issue, but were soon repulsed by Indian troops flown in when the maharaja hastily acceded to India. Kashmir was divided between both India and Pakistan along the ceasefire line, pending a plebiscite – which has never been held. An invasion by Pakistan in 1965 was aborted and ever since the issue has caused a bitter divide between the two neighbouring states, bringing them into military conflict on four occasions.

Applying the principle of geographical integrity, Nehru regained French Pondicherry by negotiation after Independence, and Portuguese Goa by force in 1961. He was less successful in fighting China over territory on the Tibetan frontier. Egalitarian and agnostic, Nehru passed laws against the injustice of the caste system, child-marriage, and the treatment of women in Hindu households, but century-old customs die hard: before his death in 1964, he asked that his ashes be scattered in the Yamuna River at Delhi and the Ganga at Allahabad, and without ritual. The mourning crowds, though, ignored his last wishes, uttering prayers and crying: 'Panditji has become immortal.'

Coming to power in the year 1966 after the brief ministry of Lal Bahadur Shastri, Indira Gandhi proved strong enough in her own right for people to stop describing her as Nehru's daughter.

In fact, she learned much from him and Gandhi: the knack for negotiating the corridors of power of the one and the ability to create a massive popular appeal of the other. She accelerated industrialisation, in particular the nuclear power industry, including a first atomic explosion in the desert in 1974. Her proudest achievement, though, was the Green Revolution that modernised wheat and rice farming to give India a surplus in food production. Old entrenched conservatism hampered her –

Indira Gandhi

often brutal and discriminatory against the poor. Birth-control programmes involving forced sterilisations were devised to check the rocketing population growth.

Indira Gandhi's tough brand of authoritarianism was highlighted during the repressive state of emergency declared in 1975. Describing it as 'disciplined democracy', she ordered mass arrests of opposition leaders who had charged her and her party with malpractice and corruption.

The electorate punished her in 1977 with three years in the wilderness, then brought her back with a huge majority. But her second term was beset with the problems of regional unrest, most notably in Assam in the northeastern region of the country, where local massacres left 3,000 dead, and in the Punjab, where Sikh militants staged violent demonstrations for greater autonomy and even independence. It was her order to the Indian Army in 1984 to attack armed militants in the Sikhs' sacred Golden Temple in Amritsar, resulting in 800 dead, that led to her assassination in Delhi five months later by two Sikh members of her security guard. Hindus then went on the rampage through Sikh communities, resulting in a round of communal violence.

Riding a wave of popular sympathy, her son, Rajiv Gandhi, and the Congress Party set out on an aggressive programme of 'modernisation'. In addition to a gas leak at the Union Carbide chemical plant that left thousands dead in Bhopal shortly before Gandhi's election to office in 1984, numerous regional conflicts at home and a somewhat schizophrenic foreign policy troubled Rajiv's term. As a result, he and his party were defeated in the elections of November 1989 by the National Front, composed of five parties including the Hindu nationalist Bharatiya Janata Party (BJP). The National Front attempted to set up a new government first with V.P. Singh and later, in 1991, with S. Chandra Shekhar as prime minister. The Congress Party regained power, however, following Rajiv Gandhi's assassination by a Tamil suicide bomber during election campaigns in 1991. P.V. Narasimha Rao, the new Prime Minister, adopted aggressive economic reforms to combat a looming financial crisis.

The BJP's role in provoking the 1992 demolition by Hindus of a mosque in Ayodhya, and the widespread violence which ensued, caused Prime Minister Rao to ban the BJP. Though this party fell into disfavour for some time, their fundamentalist agenda, shared by members of the extreme right-wing Maharashtran nationalist Shiv Sena Party, increased in popularity in subsequent years. Accusations of corruption among officials in Rao's administration in 1995 also paved the way for a comeback. The BJP eventually defeated Congress in the general elections of May 1996, winning the largest number of seats in Parliament. Represented by Prime Minister Atal Behari Vajpayee, the BJP was forced to back down, however, having failed in efforts to form a coalition government. The United Front, composed of 13 parties supported by Congress, placed H.D. Deve Gowda at the helm.

Narasimha Rao, prime minister in the early 1990s

With the backing of Congress, Prime Minister Gowda ruled until May 1997, when Congress unseated him and appointed Inder Kumal Gujral in his place. Despite the instability of the nation's government at this time, it is remarkable that in the year that India celebrated its 50th Anniversary of Independence, a Dalit (or member of an oppressed caste), K.R. Narayan, was appointed president for the first time.

In early 1998, political volatility necessitated India's first ever mid-term parliamentary elections, leading Congress to withdraw support from Prime Minister Gujral and to make Atal Behari Vajpayee of the BJP head of a multi-party coalition government. In May, Vajpayee announced the successful completion of nuclear tests, which, although touted by the Indians as a sign of their sovereignty, has complicated India's relations with its neighbours, not least Pakistan, which successfully tested its own nuclear bomb soon after.

Escalating tension between the world's two newest nuclear powers came to a head in the summer of 1999 when it emerged that Pakistani-backed militants had crossed the Line of Control in disputed Kashmir to shell Indian military positions. A full-scale battle erupted high in the mountains around the town of Kargil, ending in a decisive Indian victory.

The ensuing surge in popularity of Prime Minister Vajpayee swept him and his NDA coalition to a convincing win at the polls in 1999. But the situation in Indian Kashmir only worsened over the coming year, with frequent massacres, bombings, ambushes and suicide raids aggravating already strained relations between India and Pakistan.

However, it was the storming of the Parliament Building by Islamic militants in December 2001 that ultimately brought the two countries to the brink of all-out war. Only intense US-led diplomacy averted what would have been a catastrophic clash between the million or more men at arms who over the months afterwards lined up along the border.

Deteriorating relations between New Delhi's Hindu-dominated government and Pakistan's Islamic military rulers was mirrored by an increase in communal tension in India itself through 2002. After a train of Hindu pilgrims was allegedly attacked by a Muslim mob in Godhra, Gujarat, killing 38,

Prime Minister Manmohan Singh with Sonia Gandhi

reprisal rapes, riots and massacres erupted across the state. In the backlash, an estimated 2,000 Muslims were murdered and medieval mosques torn down. Gujarat's right-wing Hindu chief minister, Narendra Modi, rejected accusations that he had masterminded the pogrom, but it was widely reported at the time that his police had repeatedly stood by while massacres of Muslims took place.

Far from cementing the rule of Hindu extremism in India, Godhra and its aftermath seems only to have provoked a swing of support towards more secular government. Political commentators were astonished when, in May 2004, the Congress Party defeated Vajpayee's BJP-led NDA coalition in national elections. Congress leader, Sonia Gandhi – Italian-born widow of the murdered Rajiv Gandhi and heiress apparent to the country's most enduring political dynasty – was asked to form a government, but confounded supporters by refusing to take power. Instead, her finance minister, 71-year-old Manmohan Singh – an Oxford-educated Sikh economist – was sworn in as India's first non-Hindu prime minister.

Rich and Poor

Aside from the ongoing unrest in Kashmir and perennially unstable relations with Pakistan, the most urgent problems faced by India's governments in recent years have been a string of natural disasters. In 1999–2000, a super-cyclone in Orissa, drought in Rajasthan and floods in the southeast claimed millions of lives, while in January 2001, the remote region of Kutch in Gujarat was struck by a devastating earthquake that killed an estimated 40,000–60,000 people. The Asian tsunami which struck the east coast on 26 December 2004 is thought to have killed almost 20,000 people, most of them in Tamil Nadu.

The long-term impact of these disasters has fallen most heavily on the poorest inhabitants of the affected regions, hundreds of thousands of whom are still struggling to rebuild their lives. Yet their plight – and that of the millions uprooted by large-scale dam construction across the centre of the country – has attracted less attention than the economic boom being enjoyed by India's new urban elite. Lured by the low labour costs and inexhaustible supply of highly educated, English-speaking graduates, many infotech multinationals have opened offices in Bangalore, Hyderabad, Pune and Delhi, making India the world's second-largest producer of software; countless call centres, publishing firms and 'back-office' providers have followed suit.

'Out-sourcing' may be the buzz word among the country's affluent middle classes these days, but the trickle-down of benefits from the boom has yet to be felt by the rural poor who comprise four-fifths of India's inhabitants. With a population fast approaching 1.1 billion, the world's largest democracy remains unable to curb corruption in government and ensure an equitable distribution of its vast resources. Millions still lack access to safe drinking water, adequate nutrition, health care and education, while programmes to build gigantic dams, space rockets and nuclear bombs progress at pace. The quandary facing India's rulers remains how the country can continue to balance demands for security and modernisation with meeting the basic needs of its people.

Historical Landmarks

2500–1600BC Harappan (Indus Valley) Civilisation.

1500BC Aryans migrate to the Indian subcontinent from Central Asia.

563BC Birth of Siddhartha Gautama, the Buddha.

326BC Alexander the Great invades northwestern India.

c. **325BC** Chandragupta Maurya founds the Mauryan empire.

c. **260BC** King Asoka converts to Buddhism.

c. **AD320** Gupta empire is established.

c. **1200** Muslim armies conquer northern India; decline of Buddhism.

1206 Delhi sultanate is founded.

1498 Vasco da Gama reaches India.

1526 Babur overthrows Delhi sultanate, establishes Mughal empire.

1631–48 Emperor Shah Jahan builds Taj Mahal.

1642 East India Co. opens trading station at Madras (Chennai).

1690s East India Co. establishes Calcutta (Kolkata) as its main base.

1756 Nawab of Bengal attacks Calcutta; reprisals by Robert Clive consolidate British Empire in India.

1857 Indian Mutiny; India comes under direct British rule.

1885 First meeting of Indian National Congress.

1911 George V announces that the capital will be transferred to Delhi

1920–22 Mahatma Gandhi leads Non-Cooperation campaign.

1947 Independence; partition of subcontinent into India and Pakistan.

1948 Assassination of Mahatma Gandhi.

1965 Pakistan invades Kashmir.

1971 War with East Pakistan leads to creation of Bangladesh.

1974 India explodes its first nuclear bomb.

1975–77 Indira Gandhi imposes a state of emergency.

1984 Indira Gandhi is assassinated following attacks on Golden Temple.

1991 Rajiv Gandhi is assassinated.

1999 War with Pakistan-backed forces around Kargil in Indian Kashmir.

2001 Parliament Building in Delhi is stormed by Islamic militants.

2003 Kashmir ceasefire begins a thawing of relations with Pakistan.

2004 Manmohan Singh elected prime minister; tsunami hits east coast.

2005 Earthquake kills more than 1,000 people in Indian Kashmir.

2006 In Mumbai, 207 rail commuters die in terrorist bomb blasts.

WHERE TO GO

Where, indeed? This subcontinent is so rich and varied that the choice of what to see on a first visit can be daunting. Don't even think of 'doing' India the way people 'do' Europe. With some judicious selection from among the places we suggest, you can most certainly get a pretty good feel for the country in the four weeks that most visitors devote to a first trip.

Even if you have a distinct taste for improvisation and a horror of schedules and detailed itineraries, you must accept from the outset, if your time is at all limited, that travelling around India will demand a certain amount of planning. Remember, there are over one billion Indians out there, and a lot of them will be on the move at the same time as you will be, so you will at least need to make some advance reservations for hotels in principal cities and for your major plane or train journeys. This will still leave you plenty of room for getting off the beaten track and staying overnight in new and unexpected places.

GETTING AROUND

The guide is divided into the following broad sections: **Delhi**, **The North**, **Rajasthan**, **The West**, **The East** and **The South**. It's easy to pick and mix according to time and inclination. Thus, if wanting to follow the classic Golden Triangle route (Delhi, Agra, Jaipur), you'll need to refer to different sections (Delhi, The North and Rajasthan), while those wishing to follow the Ganga plain all the way from west to east will glean their information from both 'The North' and 'The East'. For international visitors the starting points are Delhi for the north, Mumbai for the west, Kolkata for the east and Chennai or Thiruvananthapuram for the south.

It's possible to overdose on cultural sights, so a selection of other attractions such as nature reserves and national parks,

Gopura detail at the Shri Meenakshi Sundeshwara temple, Madurai

beach resorts, hill stations, deserts and mountains will be part of most people's itinerary. Even if your budget allows you to fly around the country, you will never be able to cover everything, so it's best to design a 'menu' of places to see in each region.

Tourist information offices can be very helpful. You will find their guides are much more reliable than those outside the temples or palaces, but one word of warning: different tour guides will give contradictory explanations about the significance of statues as well as many different versions of legend and historical 'fact'. It would be easy to dismiss these explanations as being nonsense, but you'll understand India better if you can appreciate that what each guide is saying may in its own way be true.

Practical Hints

The HANDY TRAVEL TIPS section at the back of the book offers details on how to handle the practical side of your trip, but it's worth keeping a few points in mind when deciding where you're going in the time you have available.

The climate in India imposes its own imperatives and restrictions on your itinerary. The Himalayan regions are simply impractical in December, Delhi unbearably hot in June, and flights uncertain in the monsoon. Think of three seasons – cool, hot and wet – emphasised here because they take on a particular meaning in the Indian context. The cool season is from November to February, the ideal time for seeing most of India (except in the northern hills and mountains, where it's bitterly cold). Cool means it is pleasantly warm by day, and fresh enough for a sweater in the evening. The temperature begins to rise by mid-February. Hot, from mid-March to June, is hot as people only rarely experience it. The cities and plains in this season are definitely a bad bet, but the hill stations will be at their best. From mid-June through September, wet means monsoon-wet, not all day every day, but torrential rains occur often enough to make travel uncertain and the mosquitoes and other bugs a real nuisance. However, during this time the country is at its most green, and the monuments, especially the Taj Mahal, take on a glistening beauty.

With regard to your health *(see also page 237)*, two attitudes herald a miserable time: carelessness and hypochondria. Take elementary precautions by sticking to bottled drinks and freshly cooked food, and you won't have any serious stomach problems. An occasional touch of 'Delhi belly' is unavoidable when you're not used to the spicy food, but nothing to worry about; take it easy and drink lots of liquids, and it will pass. If you are on a short trip, you may need to take a quick-acting remedy to keep you on your feet, but if you load up with antibiotics and a host of other patent medicines, your body will never build up resistance, and the next attack will just be worse.

It is essential to protect yourself from the heat. Save your suntanning for the beach or the hotel swimming pool. Otherwise, stay out of the sun. Wear a nicely ventilated hat and keep to the shade in the street. Try to do your open-air sightseeing in the morning and late afternoon. Take a siesta after lunch. Drink plenty of liquids – in the heat, dehydration is more of a risk than an upset stomach.

The Maharaja's Palace at Mysore during Diwali

In all senses of the word, stay cool. In the first few days jet-lag, acclimatisation and culture shock may lead you to lose your temper when you see the airports, railways and hotels not organised in a way you're used to, but don't forget that John Kenneth Galbraith called it a functioning anarchy. Count to ten, and, like Delhi belly, it'll pass. Airports, railway stations and hotels can be a pain anywhere in the world these days. Indians are mostly cheerful, responding much more readily to a smile than a scowl.

The red tape can at times seem like barbed wire, but this, too, can be handled. Part of India's legacy after several centuries of bureaucracy (don't just blame the British civil service – it began long before) is an inordinate respect for the written document and the rubber stamp. Don't knock it – use it. Vouchers, passes, letters of introduction and printed business cards all work like magic when a 'confirmed' reservation has become 'unconfirmed'.

If you're travelling by train *(see page 236)* and rate comfort above improvisation, go first class with an Indrail pass. Indrail passes come in three classes, and their main advantage is that they can get you access to 'quotas' when the train is allegedly 'full'. However, travelling with an Indrail pass is a lot more expensive and doesn't always speed up booking. Indian Airlines' (<www.indian-airlines.nic.in>) *Discover India* plan offers 7, 15 or 21 days of unlimited travel, but is less economic than single tickets bought *en bloc* that you have to reconfirm at each new airport. Jet Airways (<www.jetairways.com>) offer similar multi-flight deals.

Bhil dancer in festival dress

Echoing around every office you will hear the cheerful phrase: 'No problem'. Though it rarely means exactly this, interpret it as meaning 'no catastrophe' and have a good time anyway.

A busy street in Old Delhi

DELHI

Situated on the Yamuna (Jumna) River at the western end of the great Ganga Valley, the capital was repeatedly a target for conquerors from the northwest. They each very often destroyed the work of their predecessors, but the city remains a fascinating compendium of India's imperial history.

Recent archaeological finds suggest that a site on the Yamuna may have been the home of *Mahabharata* hero Yudhishthira, dating back to 1000BC. A rock inscription from Emperor Asoka indicates that Delhi was a major point on the trade route between the northwest frontier and Bengal in the 3rd century BC.

The Tomara Rajputs made it their capital in AD736, with the name of Dhillika, and it was a focus of clan wars until the Muslims conquered it and Qutb-ud-din Aybak set up his Sultanate in 1206. Delhi was dismantled to make way for new monuments which then suffered from the devastating passage of Timur the Lame in 1398. He took away 90 elephant loads of building materials and thousands of skilled Delhi stonemasons and sculptors to build his mosque at Samarkand. With the advent of the

Mughals in 1526, Delhi alternated with Agra as the capital, and each ruler asserted his particular taste in architectural caprice.

Under the British, the town took a back seat to the ports of Calcutta, Bombay and Madras until 1911, when it became once more a proud imperial capital. No less vain than the Mughals, the new conquerors all added to New Delhi their own architectural tastes, which were a tribute to India's past but unmistakably British in overall conception.

It is possible to sign up for guided tours of the capital, which take you through a mixture of imposing ministries and embassies, modern office buildings and hotels, and along the Old Delhi of vibrant Hindu and Muslim communities crowding in on the Mughal monuments. For more orientation, visit the India Government Tourist Office on Janpath (<www.incredibleindia.org>).

Delhi of the Sultans

Start at the southern end of the city, with the **Qutb Minar**, a symbol of Islam's impact on India. Begun by Delhi's first sultan, Qutb-ud-din, and completed by his son-in-law Iltutmish, the 73m (240ft) tower was erected to celebrate the Turkish conquest of Delhi. The tower comprises four stories, each a tapering cylinder with angular and convex ribs, separated by balconies. The top of

---

Victorian Vandals

Mongols and Persians were not the only plunderers to vandalise Delhi. Most of the Red Fort's palace apartments were dismantled by the British to build army barracks after recapturing the city from the 'mutineers' in 1857. This officially sanctioned vandalism has to be understood within the context of the vindictive climate that reigned after the mutiny. Some of the more enlightened viceroys did their best to make amends in order to protect and restore India's patrimony. But Lord Curzon and other officials often had to contend with philistine circuit judges, who thought nothing of whitewashing or plastering over frescoes in a Mughal mausoleum while turning it into a rest house.

the tower is off limits, due to dangers inherent in the narrow staircase that leads to the lookout point, so the best bet for a panoramic view of the city is the top floor of one of the taller, more recent hotels.

Adjacent to the Qutb Minar, the ruined **Quwwatu'l-Islam-Masjid** (which means 'The Might of Islam') was built by local Hindu craftsmen as Qutb had no skilled Muslim labour at his disposal. The materials came from 27 Hindu and Jain temples, which had been demolished by the craftsmen's own elephants. You can see the results in the temple-pillars set on top of one another. Sculptures have been plastered over,

The Qutb Minar

but the Indian carving remains. Islamic architecture shows in the five characteristic peaked arches of the prayer-hall screen, but even here the decoration is naturalistic and Hindu in style.

In the mosque's courtyard there is a 7m (22ft) **Iron Pillar** from the 4th century, brought here by the Rajput founders of Dhillika, but nobody knows from where. Without rust after 1,600 years worth of monsoon, this monument to Garuda, the Hindu god Vishnu's winged vehicle *(vahana)*, is said to have special properties.

City of the Mughals

Due east of New Delhi's India Gate, the much-plundered 16th-century Purana Qila (Old Fort) stands on an ancient mound, now believed to mark the site of Indraprastha of the *Mahabharata* epic.

The earliest Mughal building in Delhi, the **Qal'a-i-Kuhna-Masjid**, with its minutely detailed moulding of graceful peaked arches, represents an important transition from the Turco-Afghan to the sophisticated style of the Persian-influenced Mughals. The mosque was built in the year 1541 by Sher Shah, the Emperor Babur's general in office. **Sher-Mandal**, the octagonal tower due south of the mosque, served as the general's pleasure-palace, but it was to be the death of his rival and successor, Humayun *(see below)*.

From Humayun's death came the splendid monument located in Nizamuddin, the **Tomb of Humayun**, which was built by his widow Haji Begum and was the inspiration for the Taj Mahal. It stands on a raised terrace in a set of walled-in tree-shaded lawns surrounded by hedges, but without the water once running in its channels ('rivers of life'), or the rectangular pools that were to grace the grounds of the Taj. Humayun's tomb has a remarkable charm of its own, a site for repose and serenity made from a delicate combination of materials – buff-and-red sandstone and smart, grey-trimmed white marble. With a majestic dome uniting the four octagonal kiosks over the terrace's latticed arches, this is the first fully-realised masterpiece of Mughal architecture. The numerous six-pointed stars set in the abutments of the main arches are not the Jewish Star of David but an esoteric emblem that you will see all over the country.

Death of an Emperor

Everybody thought that Emperor Humayun had kicked his opium addiction when he returned from exile in Persia to reclaim his throne in 1555. But one day in the Sher-Mandal, which he had converted into a place where he could study his books on astrology and secretly indulge his habit, he was coming down the stairs, feeling more than a little woozy, when the *muezzin* at the local mosque started calling the faithful to prayer. Legend has it that the Great Mughal tried to kneel right there on the staircase, tumbling over and fatally cracking his head.

The Red Fort

Dominating Old Delhi, the **Lal Quila** (Red Fort) was built by
Shah Jahan when he transferred the capital back to Delhi from
Agra, and was completed by 1648. Behind its ramparts, the
Delhi citadel is more a palace than a fortress, with white marble
preferred over the region's red sandstone. It is thought he used
the same architect who worked on the Taj Mahal.

From south of the fort, notice the two monumental elephants
outside the Delhi Gate. Part of the original design, they were
destroyed by Emperor Aurangzeb, who refused images suscepti-
ble to idolatry. Viceroy Lord Curzon had these replicas installed
in 1903. Enter the fort on its west side at the Lahore Gate and
you'll find yourself in a vaulted bazaar street, an idea Shah
Jahan borrowed from Baghdad. Imagine administrators and Rajput princes riding on elephants through the arcade as far as the
Naubat Khana (Drum House), where the imperial band played
and visitors were obliged to dismount.

Pass with the ghosts of these nobles and commoners through the
Drum House to the **Diwan-i-Am** (Hall of Public Audience). Here,
under a baldaquin with 40 pillars, the emperor sat cross-legged on

his throne, the 'Seat of the Shadow of God'. He held audience, surrounded by nobles, at midday, while common petitioners attended in the courtyard below. As a visitor, you can admire the inlaid stone panels of birds and flowers at the back of the hall.

Entrance to the **Diwan-i-Khas** (Hall of Private Audience) was for the privileged, by ticket only. You will find it on the left, among the palace apartments on the Yamuna River. Beautiful as it is, with carved designs on the marble columns and cusped arches, imagine it in its full glory before the ravages of Nadir Shah in 1739. His Persian troops chipped the gold out of its pillars and inlay off the ceiling, and then carted away the fabulous Peacock Throne. Above the arches you will see the inscription:

If paradise on earth there be,
'Tis here, 'tis here, 'tis here!'

Worse damage still was inflicted to the fort by the British, after they re-took it from Bahadur Shah's poorly organised defenders at the end of the 1857 uprising. Whole wings of exquisitely carved palaces were levelled and ugly brick barracks erected in their place. One of the few surviving apartments is the principal harem, **Rang Mahal** (Palace of Colour). The walls' paintings have gone and water no longer flows in its indoor Nahr-i-Bihisht (River of Paradise), but mosaics made of mirrors ornament the ceiling and walls of six boudoirs, making a galaxy of stars when candle-lit. Southernmost of the palace buildings, **Mumtaz Mahal** was part of the imperial harem and is now a small museum of Mughal artwork.

To the northwest of the Diwan-i-Khas, the **Moti Masjid** (Pearl Mosque) is the one contribution to the fort by Shah Jahan's successor, Aurangzeb. Each evening, a sound and light show at the Red Fort tells its story; details can be obtained from the India Government Tourist Office on Janpath.

Chandni Chowk, the road from the fort's Lahore Gate, was once an avenue for processions. Today, it is the main thoroughfare linking Delhi's bazaars, which sell jewellery, clothes and traditional sweetmeats.

The **Raj Ghat**, the simple memorial to Mahatma Gandhi overlooking the Yamuna River, is far in spirit from the Mughals but an integral part of Old Delhi. On lawns planted with trees donated by visiting heads of state, a square of marble marks the place where Gandhi was cremated. The platform has an inscription recording his last words – Hé Ram (Oh, God) – and nearby, a sign declares that most famous Gandhi talisman: 'Recall the face of the poorest and most helpless man whom you may have seen and ask yourself if the step you contemplate is going to be of any help to him.' There is also a museum recording the highlights of Gandhi's life. To the north is **Shanti Vana**, where members of the Nehru dynasty have been cremated.

On an outcrop of rock southwest of the Red Fort stands Shah Jahan's other great construction, the **Jama Masjid** (the great congregational 'Friday Mosque'). The inadvisability of a morning or late afternoon visit on hot days will become apparent when you see the three pyramidal flights of stairs to the gate-houses.

Eternal flame at the Raj Ghat

The 100-sq-m (1,076-sq-ft) courtyard is enclosed by long colonnades with a pavilion at each corner. The prayer hall highlights the emperor's aesthetic, in the lotus calyx on the gateway's two lantern shafts, the delicately flaring balconies on the minarets, and the stripes to emphasise the bulbous marble domes.

New Delhi

Those nostalgic for the British empire please note: Clive Road has been named Tyagaraja, Queen Victoria Road has become Rajendra Prasad, and Curzon is Kasturba Gandhi. Though the statues of British leaders have also disappeared, the British spirit remains in the city's planning. Faithful to the policy of separating the British cantonment from the Indian quarters with a railway as the barrier, the new city built for the empire's Indian seat of government is separated from Old Delhi by the line running from Amritsar to Agra. British neoclassical architecture here is mixed with elements of the Buddhist, Hindu and Mughal past, and the geometry of its plan exudes the self-confidence of the empire. As a visiting statesman once said of it: 'What splendid ruins it will make!'

The commercial hub of New Delhi is the circular arcade and bustling roundabout of **Connaught Place**. With cinemas, banks, travel agencies, restaurants and the better craft emporiums, it's a place whose new name, Indira Chowk, does not seem to have caught on. Connaught Place straddles the northeast–southwest axis that links the Jama Masjid mosque of Old Delhi to India's parliament, **Sansad Bhavan**. Designed by the famous Herbert Baker, the rather too massive, colonnaded rotunda of the parliament building is at its best illuminated at night.

The **Jantar Mantar**, set south of Connaught Place, is perhaps the strangest monument in New Delhi. It is difficult to believe that these bizarre shapes, staircases going nowhere and windows in walls without rooms were built in 1724 by a serious student, rather than in the last century by some deranged architect. It is in fact the astrologico – that is, the astronomical observatory – of Rajput Prince Jai Singh II from

India Gate

Jaipur *(see page 112)*. Its centrepiece is the right-angled triangle, Samrat Yantra (the Supreme Instrument), with a dome acting as a sun-dial, 'accurate to half a second'. In addition to this structure, he built four more – in Ujjain, Varanasi, Mathura and his native Jaipur.

Near the Jantar Mantar, you can witness the joyous atmosphere of popular Hinduism at the **Hanuman Mandir** (Temple of the Monkey God). Hanuman is a beneficent deity predating classical Hinduism, and the reason why no one would dream of harming the little langurs and macaques running around here.

The Viceroy's Residence, now the President's house, **Rashtrapati Bhavan**, has wings radiating from the great grey-blue dome of the central block and the tranquil pools and lawns of its gardens, and so bespeaks the grandeur of Britain's heyday. It looms from an artificial hill along the processional avenue, **Rajpath** (once Kingsway), which is flanked by parklands, where India holds its marches on Republic Day, 26 January. At the other end of Rajpath stands **India Gate**, the war memorial designed by Lutyens in the style of a triumphal arch that

The Jantar Mantar was built in 1724

pays tribute to 90,000 Indian Army soldiers who died in World War I. Close by the arch is a cupola that now stands empty. This once held a giant white marble statue of the British King George V, which has been transferred to the site of the coronation durbar in the far north of the city.

Museums

The **National Museum**, on Janpath (Queensway) just south of Rajpath, contains a matchless collection of antiques spanning 5,000 years of Indian history, gathered from across the subcontinent. Allow at least three hours to do it justice.

Railway buffs will surely enjoy the display of the country's early steam engines at the open-air **Rail Transport Museum**. It is situated in the diplomatic neighbourhood of Chanakyapuri, southwest of Rajpath.

Nehru Memorial Museum is devoted to Independence and the life of India's first prime minister. It is located in the house that Nehru inherited from the British Indian Army commander-in-chief on Teen Murti Road (it also houses a planetarium).

THE NORTH

This section encompasses the states of Uttar Pradesh, Punjab, Himachal Pradesh, Jammu and Kashmir and Uttaranchal. The heart of the Mughal Empire can be found at Agra, with the incomparable Taj Mahal, as well as the nearby abandoned city of Fatehpur Sikri. The holy city of Varanasi is the very soul of India, while memories of the Uprising are kept alive at Lucknow. Punjab is home to the Sikh city of Amritsar with its extraordinary Golden Temple. In the Himalayas there is the hill station of Simla and the glorious Kullu Valley; there's also Ladakh, with its Buddhist monasteries, lying beyond the passes to the north; and the Garhwal, home to Hindu holy sites such as Gangotri. And beneath all that, is the magical Corbett National Park.

Agra

Location of the Taj Mahal, **Agra** is the most popular tourist destination in India. Even if the place had nothing else, it would be worth the trip, for the Taj, as one calls it, is a 'sight' that awakens the wonder and enthusiasm of the most blasé, world-weary traveller, a sight for which no amount of stunning photography in guidebooks and magazines can adequately prepare you.

But there's plenty more. Agra was the capital of Akbar the Great, the site of his fort, of his tomb outside the city at Sikandra, and, several kilometres west at Fatehpur Sikri, of the marvellous deserted town he built to celebrate the birth of a son and which he abandoned to fight on the northwest frontier. Descendants of the craftsmen originally brought here continue a tradition in jewellery, brassware, ivory and inlaid marble.

Don't try to do Agra in one day. It is possible (and certainly better than missing it entirely), but it means you won't see much more than the Taj and, say, the fort. More important, you might miss the unique beauty of the Taj as it changes in the light of different times of day.

The first historical mention of Agra is in 1501, when Sultan Sikandar Lodi made it his capital. Babur captured it along with the Koh-i-Nur diamond, now among the British crown jewels. His grandson Akbar chose Agra for his capital over Delhi. In the 17th century, Jahangir made it a major focus of the Islamic world. His son Shah Jahan lost his taste for Agra after finishing the Taj Mahal for his wife Mumtaz-Mahal following her death. He moved the capital back to Delhi again in 1648, leaving the city's treasure to vandals (including the British) after the 1857 'Mutiny', until the viceroys organised its restoration. Today it is the effects of pollution that are taking their toll on Agra's monuments.

Taj Mahal

This is truly a monument for all seasons. There are those who swear by the sight of the **Taj Mahal** in the Sharad Purnima, the first full moon after the monsoons, a cloudless midnight in October when the light is at its clearest and also most romantic. Others love to see it in the middle of the heaviest monsoon, its marble translucent, its image blurred in the rain-stippled water channels of its gardens. But its magic is strong at any time of year, and any moment of the day. At dawn, its colour changes from milk to silver to rose-pink, and at sunset it is golden. Observe it, too, in the brilliance of midday, for then it is utterly, dazzlingly white. On nights with a full moon, the grounds stay open until midnight.

The Taj Mahal at sunset

The **gateway** to the gardens of the mausoleum can be admired as a masterpiece in its own right, with graceful marble arches, the domed kiosks on the four corner turrets, and two rows of 11 small *chattri* (umbrella-domes) just above the entrance. It provides visitors with the perfect frame for a first view of the ensemble. You will find that external photography is allowed, but it is forbidden to take pictures inside the tomb itself.

The *chharbagh* (foursquare) gardens are an integral part of the Taj Mahal, both spiritually, as the symbol of the Paradise to which Mumtaz-Mahal has ascended, and artistically, to enhance the colour and texture of the mausoleum. The dark cypresses heighten the brilliance of the monument's marble, and the water channels (on those rare occasions when they're full) meeting at a broad central viewing platform, not only provide a perfect second image, but also, with the reflection of the sky, add at dawn and sunset a subtle illumination from below.

Exquisite harmony and refined symmetry are the keynotes of the mausoleum itself. The structure is clad in miraculously white marble from the Rajasthan quarries of Makrana, achieving a magnificent texture with the subtly alternating broad and narrow slabs. Standing protectively at the four corners of the raised terrace, the minarets are, deferentially, slightly lower than the sublime central cupola. Inside, the octagonal cenotaph-chamber contains the ceremonial marble coffins of Mumtaz-Mahal and also Shah Jahan, while, as was the custom of that time, the actual bodies are entombed in another chamber direct-

---

A Marble Requiem

Mahal means palace, but in this case Taj Mahal is a diminutive of the name Mumtaz-Mahal (Exalted of the Palace) which Shah Jahan's cousin was given when she married him. Daughter of his mother's brother, she had been his constant companion long before he succeeded to the throne and was later first lady among the hundreds in his harem. In 19 years of marriage, she bore him 14 children, dying with the birth of the last in 1631.

Legend has it that Shah Jahan's beard – he was 39, one year older than his wife – turned white practically overnight when she died, and he continued to mourn for years, dressing in white on each anniversary of her death. The 12 years taken to build her mausoleum, working untiringly with his Persian architect and with craftsmen brought from Baghdad, Italy and France, may be regarded as the supreme sublimation of his grief. 'Empire has no sweetness for me now', he wrote. 'Life itself has lost all relish.'

All the same, he lived to what was then a ripe old age (74), dying from an overdose of opium and aphrodisiacs while enjoying the company of some of his many concubines.

ly below. You'll need to light a candle or use a flashlight in the cenotaph-chamber because daylight barely filters through the beautiful marble trellis-screens *(jalis)*.

Sadly, vandals removed all the tomb's treasures, but they did leave the gentle beauty of roses and poppies in rich in-laid stones of onyx, green chrysolite, carnelian and var-iegated agate. The mausoleum is flanked by two almost iden-tical red buildings, to the west a mosque, to the east a guest pavilion. Each is a perfect viewpoint: try the pavilion at sunrise and the mosque at sunset. But go around the back of the Taj, too, to the ter-

Exquisite inlay work at the Taj

race which overlooks the Yamuna River. This boasts a view as far as Agra Fort. At dawn, one of the best (and cheaper) view-points is from the opposite bank of the river, where Shah Jahan planned a mirror image Taj made of jet-black marble. Boatmen line up to ferry visitors across.

Agra Fort
Built by Akbar in 1565, a more embattled period than during Shah Jahan's construction of the Red Fort in Delhi, **Agra Fort** ◀ was conceived as a citadel with a moat on three sides and a river on the fourth. Pleasure palaces were a secondary consideration, and were in fact mostly additions by Akbar's successors.

The entrance from the south, at Amar Singh Gate, takes you up a ridged elephant's ramp, sloped to slow down any potential attackers. Pass into the long quadrangle of the pillared **Diwan-i-**

Am (Hall of Public Audience). It was here that Captain William Hawkins handed Emperor Jahangir a special letter of introduction from King James I. Due north is Shah Jahan's **Moti Masjid** (Pearl Mosque). Climb the narrow staircase to the roof of the mosque for a fine view of the fort.

Just off the northeast corner of the Diwan-i-Am, the harem had its very own mosque, **Nagina Masjid**, a Hindu temple, the **Mandir Raja Ratan** (built in 1768 during the Jat occupation), and between the two a bazaar where merchants sold silks and jewels. Near the hammam (baths), the **Diwan-i-Khas** (Hall of Private Audience) has rich carving and inlaid marble. The crack in the marble throne came from a British cannonball in 1857. As in Delhi's fort, most of the private palace apartments face the

Agra Fort

Yamuna River. Among the most charming are the arcaded loggia and the gilt-roofed pavilions of the **Khas Mahal** (Private Palace). A minute staircase led to the **Musamman Burj**, the pavilion of the emperor's chief wife. It is also popularly known as the 'Prisoner's Tower' for Aurangzeb imprisoned his father Shah Jahan here, allowing him a view of his beloved Taj Mahal.

The **Palace of Jahangir** is built around a square court with arches. There are Hindu motifs on the ceiling in the main hall, and in one on the western side: peacocks holding snakes in their beaks, for example.

On the river bank opposite the fort is the **Tomb of**

Itimad-ud-Daulah, overshadowed by the Taj Mahal. This mausoleum was built 15 years earlier by Jahangir's wife, Nur Jahan, for her father, who served as Mughal *wazir* (prime minister). There's a fragile elegance to the white marble pavilion's silhouette, with a cupola and four octagonal turrets, topped by domed kiosks. The fine lattice-work on the arches and windows is superb, but its outstanding feature is the marble inlay, which is even more abundant than in the Taj, and better preserved.

Akbar's mausoleum is located at Sikandra, 10km (6 miles) north of Agra. Although lacking the grandeur of the Taj, the tomb complex presents an arresting spectacle, its huge south gate surmounted by four tapering minarets. Inside, the grounds surrounding the mausoleum itself are filled with grazing black buck and troupes of tame langur monkeys. The best view is from the top of the gateway. On the cenotaph are the 99 names of Allah.

Fatehpur Sikri

In a country of crowded cities, it makes a refreshing change to travel 37km (22 miles) southwest of Agra to an outcrop on which stands the citadel of **Fatehpur Sikri**, briefly Akbar's imperial capital.

Fatehpur, planned as a capital with Agra as a fallback position in case of attack, is protected on three sides by ramparts measuring about 6km (4 miles). On the fourth side is an artificial lake stretching 8km (5 miles) to the Rajasthan border, never sufficient, apparently, for the needs of the citadel, and so one of the probable reasons why Akbar did not settle here permanently (the explanation most often advanced is that its water supply was inadequate and polluted with salt). Built by the architects working on the Agra Fort, the citadel adds the darker red stone of the mountain ridge to the usual pink sandstone of this area.

Entering via the **Agra Gate**, at the northeast corner, one passes on the right the *karkhanas* (workshops) where carpenters, weavers and stonemasons worked.

In the **Diwan Khana-i-Am**, the courtyard used for public audiences, Akbar dispensed his justice while attended by an executioner with instruments of torture and death. The sight of the two of them was felt to be an effective means of getting at the truth. At the foot of the colonnade is a big stone tethering-ring for an elephant whose job it was to crush condemned criminals to death.

Go through the pavilion to the **Daulat Khana** (Abode of Fortune) on the south side of the courtyard, a palace of which the most striking feature is the Hindu nature of its decoration: carved pedestals with stylised elephant heads as capitals and sculpted stone screens.

In the southeast corner of the courtyard is the **Turkish Sultana's House**, or Hujra-i-Anup Talao (the Chamber of the Peerless Pool); animals covering every wall panel and pillar create the illusion of woodwork rather than stone. Fatehpur is the subject of many colourful stories in which it is impossible to establish a historian's 'truth'. For instance, in the centre of the

---

Name-Calling

The rise and fall of Fatehpur Sikri is the perfect illustration of Akbar's impulsive personality. At the end of 1568, the emperor was 26 and still without a male heir. At Sikri he met a Sufi mystic, Shaikh Salim Chishti, who promised him, given the proper spiritual dedication, not one, but three sons.

'In return for your friendship and grace', said the emperor, 'I'll protect and preserve you.'

Unmoved, the Sufi replied: 'You can name your first son after me.'

The following August, a boy was born. He was duly named Salim (later Jahangir). Overjoyed, Akbar decided to move his capital to Sikri, then embarked on a successful military campaign and came back to add the name of Fatehpur (City of Victory). By 1581 he had abandoned Fatehpur. Only the family of Shaikh Salim Chishti remained, near the shrine Akbar had built for them. Today, 16 generations later, they are still here, but there is no sign of Akbar's people.

The abandoned city of Fatehpur Sikri

courtyard is the **Pachisi Court**, a huge chessboard for the game of *pachisi*, where Akbar and his friends are said to have used human 'pieces' – each player using a team of four slave girls in different costumes.

Also, Akbar is said to have come to the **Astrologer's Pavilion**, in the northwest corner of the court, for a daily dose of forecasts from the house-esoteric. The emperor is known to have consulted a whole panel of experts from Hindu and Muslim schools of astrology. Just behind this is the **Treasury Pavilion**, where you can imagine Akbar seated on cushions under the arches and counting the imperial money. The pavilion was known as Ankh Michauli (Blind Man's Buff), because it was where Akbar was thought to have played 'hide-and-seek' with his wives.

The purpose of the **Diwan-i-Khas** is hotly disputed: it is not necessarily the hall of private audience that its name implies. Dominated by a great central pillar supporting bridges to a balcony, some claim it was here that Akbar held his famous debates with Jesuits, Brahmins, Parsis, Sufi mystics, and Jain and Buddhist monks – the sages arguing while Akbar sat listening atop his pillar, or striding majestically around the bridges and balcony hurling his questions at his listeners. Others insist that it was just a storehouse for jewels. Truth here, even more than beauty, is in the eye of the beholder.

Walk across the courtyard to the beautiful five-tiered **Panch Mahal**, a palace with the Persian system of ventilation known as *badgir* (wind tower): without walls on three sides, it is open for the breezes to sweep in. Each floor is supported on columns diminishing from 84 at ground level to four on the roof. Notice that no two columns on the ground floor are alike. Be careful on the steep climb to the top, but you will find it is well worth it for the wonderful view across the citadel, particularly the palaces of the imperial harem to the southwest. It is thought that Akbar used to entertain his consorts in the topmost pavilion.

The harem's principal residence is **Jodha Bhai's Palace** – built for Akbar's Hindu wife, the first royal spouse not required to convert to her husband's Islamic faith – and was Akbar's

The Panch Mahal, where Akbar entertained his consorts

favourite residence at Fatehpur. It has one side screening out the summer heat while the other is open to the cooler breezes. Its most cherished feature is the turquoise ceramic tiled roof in the north and south wings.

Fatehpur's **Jama Masjid** (the Friday Mosque), at the south end of the citadel up on its mountain ridge, was the very first of the open courtyard-style mosques that became characteristic of all Mughal cities. Notice the carved central mihrab (the recess marking the direction

Stone screen (jali) at the Tomb of Shaikh Salim Chishti

of Mecca). However, the jewel of the red stone courtyard is the marble-clad **Tomb of Shaikh Salim Chishti**. Its facade features black calligraphy; in the cenotaph-chamber there are pretty painted flowers. Originally a more simple monument, its white marble 'skin' was the addition of a very grateful Jahangir who, without the mystic Shaikh Salim Chishti, might never have seen the light of day *(see page 82)*.

Flanking the southern side of the complex, the mighty **Buland Darwaza** (Great Gate) forms an appropriately grand entry and exit point for the imperial city. It was erected in 1576 to celebrate Akbar's triumphant conquest of Gujarat and rises to a height of 54m (177ft). Visible for kilometres, an inscription from the Koran is carved over the archway. It reads:

Said Jesus son of Mary (Peace Be Upon Him): the world is but a bridge. Pass over without building houses on it. He who hopes for one hour hopes for eternity; the world is an hour – spend it in prayer for the rest is unseeen.

The Imambaras at Lucknow

Lucknow

As a logical stopover on your way to Varanasi (coming from Delhi or from Kolkata), **Lucknow** is worth a visit for its special place in the history of India's determined fight for Independence – a focus of the Uprising of 1857 *(see page 43)*. It also holds some extraordinary buildings dating from the era when it was the capital of an opulent, refined Muslim dynasty – the kingdom of Avadh, or Oudh.

The site of a bloody siege in which more than 3,000 Europeans (among them 1,400 non-combatants) held out for five months against an army of mutinous sepoys, the **British Residency** – today preserved as a monument – initially commemorated British resistance, but since Independence it has been visited by Indians interested in this relic of their own struggle for self-rule.

On a lawn surrounded by 24 palm trees, a cenotaph pays tribute to Chief Commissioner Sir Henry Lawrence, who was killed during the attack. An obelisk here honours 'Native Officers and Sepoys, who died…nobly performing their duty'. Indians comprised half the 1,700 troops defending the Residency. A little museum inside illustrates the history of the siege, with a model of the first Residency as well as rusty cannons and cannonballs, and prints, photos and letters.

Down by the river, a short walk away, is the **Martyrs' Memorial**, inaugurated in 1957 on the centenary of the Uprising to honour those who fought for India's independence.

Lucknow, with its 18th- and 19th-century mosques, used to be a Muslim stronghold; although the size of its community has now dwindled to only 30 percent of the city's population, it is one of the two most important Indian centres of Shia doctrine, the other being Mumbai. Of the crumbling monuments that remain from this final flowering of high Muslim culture in India, the **Bara Imambara** and nearby **Hussainabad Imambara** are the grandest – fairytale palaces of onion-domes, graceful arches and minarets. Their exhuberant architecture testifies to the considerable decadence and refinement for which the Nawabs of Avadh are chiefly remembered. Sadly, both are in a parlous state of disrepair, as are the city's other great monuments, **Daula's Mosque** and the ornamental victory arch known as the **Rumi Darwaza**.

Sacred Confluence

One of the most sacred places of Hinduism is **Allahabad**, 204km (127 miles) southeast of Lucknow via Kanpur. Here the Yamuna flows into the Ganga. Hindus believe the mythical and invisible River Saraswati joins the Ganga at this point. Allahabad is known as 'Tirth Raj', the king of pilgrimage places. At the sacred confluence a religious fair, the *Magh Mela*, is held each January and February, and once every 12 years the greatest religious festival of northern India, the *Mahakumbha Mela*, takes place. To bathe at the confluence at the most sacred times is said to wash away the sins of many births; in 2001 an estimated 66 million people bathed here. Rowing boats will take you to the spot where the milky waters of the Ganga meet the blue waters of the Yamuna.

On the eastern side of Lucknow in the district of Hazratganj, you can also visit the flamboyant **Shah Najaf Imambara**, whose delightful interior harbours the tomb of Ghazi-udin-Haidar (Nawab of Avadh who died in 1827). Nearby stands one of India's most famous public schools, **La Martinière**. started by a French adventurer in 1761. Its appearance, traditions and curriculum have altered little since the departure of the British.

Varanasi

One thing is certain: you cannot begin to fathom the mystery of India without a visit to **Varanasi**. Not that this old city will 'explain' everything – in fact, its dramatic confrontations of life and death on the Ganga River, and of scholarship and superstition, may only mystify you even further – but the city's aura of sanctity is so overwhelming that it supercedes any need for rational explanations. Perhaps the Muslim conquerors once perceived the Hindus' reverence for Varanasi as a threat – there is no temple in this 3,000-year-old city dating from before the 18th century – but later it became a holy city for Muslims, too, with Emperor Aurangzeb even trying to rename it Muhammadabad.

The name Varanasi, misheard by Europeans as Benares, is derived from its site between the tributaries of the life-giving holy Ganga River, the Varuna and the Asi. The god

The ghats at Varanasi

Shiva is said to have poured the river down on the plains from the Himalayas; this mythical story leads Hindus to believe that Varanasi is the oldest city in the world.

Probably founded by the Indo-Aryans around 1000BC, the city was established from earliest times as a famous seat of learning for Hindu thinkers, theologians, philosophers and poets alike. It has remained ever since a centre of the Hindu sciences. It was just outside Varanasi that Buddha's disciples gathered in the 6th century BC to hear his sermon at the Deer Park of Sarnath. Since then, Jain monks, Muslims and Sikhs have proclaimed it a holy city, building monasteries, mosques and temples here.

The Ghats

The stone-stepped embankments leading down to the Ganga River are the gathering place of more than 250,000 pilgrims a year. To see the day unfold at the ghats, you must rise before dawn to join the pilgrims. Holy men and women are up and about, busily chanting 'Ganga Mai ki jai!' – 'Praise be to Mother Ganga!'

Some are *sannyasi*, itinerant ascetics who have abandoned their homes and walked from as far as the far south of India to stand on the ghats and pray, to bathe and drink the waters of the holy river, or just to sit and meditate on this supreme moment of their religious lives. Even the most aged and infirm travel here to die, for nothing is more blessed for a devout Hindu than to have one's ashes scattered in the great waters of Varanasi and thus be released from the eternal cycle of rebirth.

Practically all roads in town lead down to the **Dasaswamedh Ghat**, where Brahma the Creator is said to have made a ritual sacrifice of 10 horses. At the top of the steps, holy men known as 'Pandas' sit under their bamboo umbrellas chanting mantras

---

Not by Faith Alone

It is hard to convince the faithful that the Ganga River is not pure. For centuries, those bodies not permitted for religious reasons to be cremated on the ghats – including babies and victims of cholera – have been dropped in the river while people bathe in and drink the water nearby.

Many firmly believe that the Ganga grants self-purification, which is reinforced for some by chemical analysis revealing a 0.05 percent sulphur content to conquer the bacteria. While faith has provided many bathers with a strong psychosomatic weapon against contamination, many of the people living permanently by the Varanasi ghats suffer from gastrointestinal diseases.

To combat pollution caused to the Ganga from dead bodies, sewage and raw industrial waste, a multi-million campaign is finally under way. For the Indian government, faith needs a little help.

Boatmen on the Ganges at Varanasi

and offering, for a coin or grains of rice, either sandalwood paste, flowers, or water from the Ganga.

At the water's edge, you can rent a boat and go into midstream for a view of the impressive skyline, which features many Hindu temples, tapering sanctuary towers, Muslim minarets and Mughal domes. In the 5km (3 miles) between her tributaries, the Ganga inscribes a crescent, turning north, as it is suggested, for one last gesture of farewell to her sacred home in the Himalayas before descending east towards the Bay of Bengal. You can ask your boatman to take you further upstream to the **Asi Ghat** before doubling back as far as the **Panchganga**.

Notice how the ritual ablutions, which are highly elaborate when performed by a learned Brahmin, usually involve a kind of crouching movement completed at least three times in the water. Women, you will notice, bathe in full sari. You'll see plenty of soap and shampoo and, on the **Dhobi Ghat**, laundry-washing, too. After all, Mother Ganga, however sacred, is also just a river. Out on stone platforms, young men perform gymnastics, part of a devout self-discipline known as danda.

Cremation in progress at the Manikarnika

Those people who might at first be reluctant to confront the omnipresence of death along the river will be impressed by the simple dignity of the funeral rites here. Families bring their dead for their cremation to the holiest of Varanasi ghats, **Manikarnika**. The body, in a white shroud, is carried on a bier of bamboo to the river's edge, where a few drops of Ganga water are poured into the lips of the dead. The body is placed on a pyre of perfumed sandalwood, which is then set alight.

Jai Singh's observatory and learning temple, the **Scindia Ghat**, is at **Man Mandir Ghat**. The **Alamgir Masjid** rises behind the sacred **Panchganga Ghat**, said to be the mythical confluence of four Ganga subterranean tributaries.

The Town

The Chawk (bazaar) is famous for its perfumes, silks and brassware. Look out for the gilded **Golden Temple of Vishwanath**, the holiest temple of Varanasi, forbidden to non-Hindus. You can view it from the building opposite before going behind the temple to see the sacred bull, stained deep vermilion by the libations of its worshippers. The Varanasi Hindu University has an **Art Museum** with a superb collection of 16th-century Mughal miniatures, considered superior to the national collection in Delhi.

Sarnath

Now a suburb of Varanasi, which is located about 10km (6 miles) out of town, Sarnath is where Buddha gave his famous Deer Park sermon (the veritable foundation of the religion) to five disciples around the year 530BC *(see page 19).*

It quickly became a leading pilgrimage site, attracting devout Buddhists from many Eastern regions including Japan, China and Southeast Asia as it still does today. Emperor Asoka commanded his edict-pillars to be built within the monasteries and *stupas* (hemispherical sculptures symbolising Buddha's Enlightenment), of which he had thousands constructed. But just like Varanasi, Sarnath suffered at the hands of Qutb-ud-din in 1194. Today the ruins have been well restored; they are accompanied by an excellent museum of Buddhist sculpture.

On the west side of the road coming out of Varanasi, you'll find the **Chaukhaudi Stupa**, built by a Gupta king in the 5th century AD. The octagonal tower that rises out of the top of the structure was added to mark the passage of the Emperor Humayun after his defeat in the 1540s. The remains of seven red-brick monasteries dating from the 3rd century BC to the 9th century AD can be discerned among the ruins in a pretty setting of flowers and sacred neem trees. Since its bricks were used to build houses in the town, only a platform of the Main Shrine, which once marked Buddha's dwelling place during his stay at Sarnath, remains.

West of the shrine, surrounded by an iron railing, are the stump and fragments of **Asoka's Pillar**, which was once over 15m (48ft) high. Notice how the shine of the granite has withstood the elements for over 2,200 years. Its inscription warns against the dissidence that could upset the important national unity under his leadership: 'No one shall cause division in the Order of Monks.'

The dominant feature of these ruins is the 45m- (146ft-) high, cylindrical **Dhamekh Stupa**, built in the 5th century AD, which is believed by many to mark the ancient site of Buddha's most famous sermon. Below the eight empty niches, notice the beautiful frieze of fine floral and geometrical patterns interspersed with pretty birds and small seated Buddhas. If you should have a pair of binoculars, they will come in handy here: take a close look at the fine craftsmanship in this work of art.

Visitors will take delight in the **Museum**, which is a treasure-trove of superb early Indian sculpture dating from the 3rd century BC to the 5th century AD. Greeting you as you enter the museum is its famous masterpiece, the lion capital of Asoka's pillar, a high point of the distinctive art of the Mauryan empire. Four vigorous lions stand back to back atop a frieze of animals comprising a horse, an elephant, a bull and a smaller lion, each of them separated by a Wheel of Law, resting on the inverted lotus that once connected it to the pillar. Against the wall is the Wheel of Law that originally rose above the lions. As a gentle counterpoint to this, and sculpted some 700 years later, a cross-legged Buddha with a finely chiselled halo was added.

Amritsar

The magnificent **Golden Temple**, holiest shrine of the Sikh faith, stands in the centre of **Amritsar**, capital of Indian Punjab. Built by Guru Arjan Dev in the 16th century, the heart of the complex is the ornately gilded Harmandir, whose domes and lotus-shaped roof are plastered entirely in pure gold leaf. Every Sikh aims to make at least one pilgrimage to the shrine in their lifetime, but its doors are open to all and many foreign visitors regard their tour here as a highlight of their trip: come early in the morning or around sunset, when the

> **From Amritsar, why not travel to the India-Pakistan border at Wagah? The Lowering of the Flag ceremony is one of the best free shows in the subcontinent, taking place just before sunset each evening. Guards on both sides strut their stuff in quite extraordinary fashion.**

The Golden Temple at Amritsar

gold colour, reflected in the waters of the **Amrit Sarovar** (Pool of Immortality Giving Nectar), is most sublime. The exotic spectacle is perfectly complemented by the live devotional music emanating from inside the Harmandir, where the Sikh holy book, the *Guru Granth Sahib*, is enshrined.

In the 1980s, the Golden Temple became infamous as the site of two bloody sieges when Sikh militants agitating for an independent homeland fought pitched battles with the Indian Army. Thousands died in what Sikhs still regard as terrible desecrations of their most sacred site. Indira Gandhi, who ordered the first attack on the temple (code-named 'Operation Blue Star'), was soon after murdered as an act of revenge by her Sikh bodyguards.

Amritsar is no stranger to mass violence. In 1919, it witnessed one of India's most appalling massacres, when British troops, under the command of General Dyer, opened fire on peaceful demonstrators at **Jallianwalla Bagh** gardens, killing between 400 and 1,500 innocent people. A memorial and martyrs' gallery at the site, not far from the Golden Temple, commemorates the atrocity, which kick-started Gandhi's movement for Home Rule.

Detail of Nek Chand's Rock Garden in Chandigarh

Chandigarh

This modern city en route to Simla was planned in 1950 by Swiss-French architect Le Corbusier, invited by the Indian government to create a new capital for the post-Partition Punjab on a windy plain at the foot of the Himalayas. With British associate Maxwell Fry designing most of the housing, Le Corbusier created the leading public buildings and laid out a town of spacious boulevards and sweeping tree-lined avenues, inspired at least in part by Lutyens' ideas for New Delhi, and blessedly uncongested by growing traffic. He planned the town on the principle of the human body, with the government buildings of the **Capitol** and university at its head, the commercial town centre at its heart, and the outlying industrial districts as its limbs.

While some hail Le Corbusier's grand design as one of the greatest influences on 20th-century architecture, Chandigarh has its fair share of detractors. Many still criticise its appearance as 'un-Indian' and the predominance of concrete as not only unsightly but also ill-suited to the intense heat of the Haryana plains. In the **Assembly** building for parliament, the **Secretariat** administrative block, the vaulted **High Court** and the smaller **Governor's Residence**, you can see huge slabs of concrete-like weathered granite from the nearby mountains. The buildings boast both geometric and amorphous shapes, with bright colours visible behind the sub-breaker grills.

Chandigarh's other chief attraction, in fact the most visited tourist destination in the state of Indian Punjab, is its extraordinary **Rock Garden**. Begun in 1965 by a Public Works Department road inspector named Nek Chand, the site comprises a maze of walled enclosures, grottos and flying walkways filled with outlandish sculptures of human figures and animals fashioned entirely from junk. It was originally intended as a small garden but Nek Chand got carried away and his labour of love has since mushroomed into a giant 10-hectare (25-acre) complex, with thousands of statues made from discarded ceramic, rubber, shattered bangles, scrap metal and industrial plastic. Many of the forms were inspired by India's distinctive tribal art. For a preview, go to: <www.nekchand.com>.

Simla

Now the capital of Himachal Pradesh, the town of **Simla** was built back in the early years of the 19th century when the British colonial settlers were desperately searching for a summer refuge from the heat of the plains.

At an altitude of 2,130m (6,755ft), this was once the place where a religious ascetic offered cool spring water to the numerous weary and thirsty travellers coming out of the Himalayas. Some of these trekkers were British troops returning from the war with the Gurkhas of Nepal in 1819. They came back to build mountain retreats, as well as regular little cottages or perhaps an occasional mansion. From 1832 onwards, after Governor-General Lord William Bentinck spent a happy summer here, it became the most prestigious hill station. The British viceroys made it their summer capital, including Lord Mountbatten who pondered the last details of Independence and Partition here in 1947.

The old reasons to head for the hills still make a trip to Simla valid, even if the old viceregal glamour has long gone. The air here is sweet, cool and clear, and the pleasure of the quaint English atmosphere remains, along with some lovely walks into the surrounding mountains. However, you should expect large crowds of Indian holidaymakers during the April–May summer break.

In town, visitors can retrace the favourite promenades along the **Mall** and see the old administrative offices of the **Ridge**. The place at which these two meet is what Kipling called 'Scandal Point'. At the eastern end of the Mall you can see the **Gaiety Theatre**, one-time home of the Simla Amateur Dramatic Company, which is famous for its productions of Victorian drama and Edwardian operetta.

Highjinks in the Hills

The British established hill stations wherever they could find a suitable area at a reasonably accessible altitude: for Madras, Ootacamund (Ooty) in the Nilgiri Hills; for Bombay, Mahabaleshwar and Matheran in the Western Ghats; and for Delhi and Calcutta, there was a choice in the Himalayas of Simla, Mussoorie, Darjeeling and many more. In the general relief at escaping the hell of the summer heat, they managed, in the classical British manner, to be very proper on the surface and nicely naughty underneath.

In these last bastions of the British Raj, class inevitably reared its head; each of the hill stations, like seaside resorts back home, had their own cachet. Senior officers made so-called poodle-faking stations off limits to subalterns, who were not permitted to watch their superiors poodle-faking with other men's wives. For, as Rudyard Kipling put it:

> Jack's own Jill go up the hill
> To Muree or Chakrata.
> Jack remains and dies in the plains
> And Jill remarries soon after.

The **Ridge** leads past the Neo-Gothic, Anglican **Christ Church**, where the bells are made from the brass of cannons captured from the Sikhs. At the end of the Ridge, you'll find the baronial pile of **Viceregal Lodge**, now used by the Institute for Advanced Studies. You can imagine rickshaws pulling up onto the grounds of the ivy-covered grey stone mansion for one of the viceroy's banquets, and this is of course where Mountbatten, Gandhi, Nehru and Jinnah held their crucial negotiations in the run-up to Partition in the 1940s. Peer into the grand hall, which has an elegant fireplace, a coffered ceiling and a majestic staircase.

Simla, once the summer capital of British Viceroys

The most popular walk out of Simla begins just behind Christ Church, from where a lane strikes steeply up to the **Jakhu Temple**. Famous for its monkeys, it is also a good vantage point for magnificent early-morning views of the distant Himalayas.

The Kullu Valley

The Kullu Valley on the River Beas, at an altitude of 1,200m (3,900ft), is renowned for apple orchards, beautiful scenery, wooden temples, and its music and dances. It offers scope for trekking, climbing, rafting and angling. **Kullu** itself has fewer attractions to detain travellers than places further up the valley. However, there are two temples in the town that are worth seeing: the Raghunathji temple, the chief deity of the valley, and the cave-temple of Vaishno Devi. Kullu really comes to life during the Dussehra festival, when tourists and locals flood into the town to see the spectacular processions of golden temple deities. Accommodation should be booked well in advance.

The most remarkable temple of the valley is **Bijli Mahadeva**, 8km (5 miles) southeast of Kullu town. It is built of large blocks of stone without the use of cement, and its 20m- (65ft-) high flagstaff is reputed to attract lightning, which, according to local legend, is an expression of divine blessing. Each time the flagstaff is struck by lightning, the Siva lingam (phallic symbol) inside the temple is shattered. It is put back together by the priest and stands until another flash repeats 'the miracle'.

The road from Kullu to Manali runs along the rushing torrents of the Beas River. It is flanked by lofty mountains and spreading forests. Near Katrain is the small town of **Naggar**, where the Castle Hotel is said to be haunted. The town has been made famous by the late Russian painter Nicholas Roerich, whose gallery can be seen here.

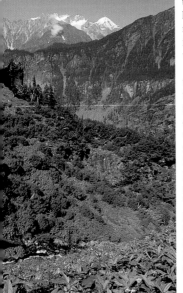

Trekking country around Manali

Manali is circled by beautiful glades of deodars and flowering horse chestnuts. It is an ideal place for walks, climbs, treks and picnics. It was an important trading centre, and in recent years has become a popular resort for Indian honeymooners, as well as Western and Israeli tourists. The town is split into two parts: the new town is where the bus-stand and most of the hotels are, while along The Mall (main street) and over the Manalsu River is the more atmospheric old village, where you can find accommodation in traditional houses. The Hindu Dhungri Temple, dedicated to the goddess Hidimba, is believed to be more than 1,000 years old, while Manali's large Tibetan population has built two new *gompas* (monasteries).

Three kilometres (2 miles) up the valley from Manali are the hot springs of **Vashisht**. The temple complex here has separate outdoor baths for men and women. The Kullu Valley ends as the road passes the ski resort of Solang and winds up through rocky ranges to the **Rohtang Pass**, gateway to the enchanting Lahaul and Spiti valleys. Marking the line of the Great Himalayan Watershed, it forms a stark divide between the lush Kullu Valley and the arid mountains beyond, which lie in the vast rainshadow of the world's highest range of peaks.

Dharamsala

West of Manali in the beautiful Kangra Valley is **Dharamsala**, at the foot of the Dhauladhar Range. Consisting of a lower and an upper town, its altitude varies from 1,000 to 2,000m (3,250 to 6,500ft). Upper Dharamsala, better known as **McLeodganj**, is the home of His Holiness the Dalai Lama and the Tibetan Government in Exile. The large Tibetan population supports many organisations, including TIPA (Tibetan Institute of Performing Arts), which preserves and arranges performances of traditional Tibetan music and dance, particularly the drama, *lhamo*. In the lower town is the **Museum of Kangra Art**, housing a collection of miniature paintings and other local artefacts.

The nearby ancient town of **Kangra** is well known for its temples – whose riches were plundered by a number of invaders – the most popular being the one dedicated to the goddess Vajresvari. Also worth visiting is Kangra's fort, once the palace of the local Katoch kings, with an outstanding view over the valley below.

Kashmir

The Vale of Kashmir, 1,700m (5,000ft) above sea level, has historically offered much-needed respite for conquerors and travellers alike. With its blessed meadows, forests, full fruit orchards and lakes, it remains the undisputed treasure of South Asia. Unfortunately, continuing tensions between India and Pakistan in the region have rendered Kashmir a dangerous place for travellers.

Srinagar

The heart of Kashmir's capital is built along the banks of the serpentine Jhelum River on the southern shore of the lakes. Few monuments have survived its troubled history, but the city's beauty lies in its numerous tranquil lakes and gardens. On the western shore of Dal Lake is the large white dome and minarets of **Hazratbal Masjid**, famous for its relic, the hair of the beard of the prophet Muhammad. There are two small squares of land that rise up out of the lake: Sonalank, Akbar's Golden Island to the north, and Ruplank, Silver Island, to the south.

> **Visitors should not visit Kashmir. Despite a thawing in relations between India and Pakistan, negotiations on the future of the region and even an opening of the border for Kashmiris, the battle between Kashmiri separatists and the Indian government rages on. No matter what tourist touts elsewhere in the country may tell you (and however persuasive their sales patter), this remains an exceptionally dangerous part of the country.**

The **Mughal Gardens** are on the eastern shore of Dal Lake. For Jahangir, if the Islamic idea of paradise had any meaning, it was here, amid the staggered terraces, tranquil pools, waterfalls and trees, looking out over the lake against the backdrop of the Himalayas. Jahangir's favourite was the **Shalimar Bagh**, laid out in the year 1616. A white marble pavilion on the first terrace was used for public audiences, the second was a private pavilion, the third – made from black marble – accommodated the harem, and the fourth was strictly reserved for the emperor's private use.

Home cooking in Zanskar

Three kilometres (2 miles) to the south, **Nishat Bagh** was created in 1633 by Jahangir's *wazir* (prime minister) and brother-in-law, Asaf Khan. It is the largest of the gardens, with 12 terraces and lined with fine cedars and cypresses. It has a magnificent view of the lake beyond.

Ladakh

Although officially within the boundries of Jammu-Kashmir state, the remote Himalayan region of **Ladakh** is a world apart, in every sense. Encircled by some of the world's highest mountains, the geography and culture of the 'Land of High Passes' has more in common with neighbouring Tibet than Muslim Kashmir. The majority of its inhabitants are Buddhists, and from the moment you first enter the region, the brightly coloured prayer flags and monasteries perched on hillsides of parched scree reinforce the impression that you have arrived on the margins of Indian influence.

Only opened to tourists in 1975, Ladakh is centred on the stunning Indus Valley, with a base altitude of around 3,500m (10,500ft). Along its floor, a string of picturesque villages cower

Tikse Monastery

beneath vast, ice-capped mountains. These form an all but impregnable barrier to the monsoon clouds sweeping north off the Indian plains, with the result that rainfall is minimal. Ladakhis survive primarily on a single crop of barley, watered by snow-melt channelled through terraced fields.

For thousands of years, the Indus Valley formed an important trade artery connecting Central Asia and Tibet with Kashmir and the Indian lowlands. Along it, tea, silk, pashmina, semi-precious stones – and the Buddhist religion – was imported in caravans of yaks and ponies. The fragile – and still disputed – borders with China and Pakistan that now enclose Ladakh have effectively blocked these ancient trans-Himalayan routes, but the region still thrives as an important military base and tourist destination.

With Kashmir effectively off limits, this is now the most accessible and visited of the high Himalayan areas in India. You can travel here by road from Manali *(see page 100)* – a stupendous two-day journey through some of the world's most breathtaking scenery – or fly direct to the Ladakhi capital, Leh, from Delhi. Aside from the awesome landscape, the main incentives to trek here are the beautiful Buddhist monasteries in and around the Indus Valley, and the chance to experience this last pocket of traditional mountain culture at close quarters.

Despite its essential remoteness, **Leh** is a developed town boasting most modern amenities: hotels and guesthouses, restaurants, cafés, travel agents, internet access and the world's highest domestic airport. Spilling from the foot of a ruined Tibetan-style palace, Leh's broad bazaar and jam of ancient mud houses looks south across the Indus Valley to the snowy peaks of the Stok Kangri massif.

Trekking in Ladakh

Thanks to the ongoing political unrest in Kashmir, Ladakh has superceded its neighbour as the northwest Himalaya's top trekking destination. Dozens of agencies are on hand in Leh to arrange ponies, guides, cooks and porters for a range of routes of various lengths through the rugged terrain surrounding the Indus Valley. All involve long, gruelling ascents of high passes that will expose you to the risk of altitude sickness, but the rewards are wonderful views across the Himalayas and the chance to visit traditional Buddhist villages lying days, or weeks, away from the road.

Deservedly the most popular route you can tackle from Leh is the Markha Valley trek, beginning at Spitok and ending at Hemis (or vice versa). This superb circuit takes six to eight days and should be attempted only once you're well acclimatised to the altitude. A shorter, easier alternative (practicable even in winter) is Likkir to Temisgang, along an ancient caravan route.

Serious trekkers wishing to walk south towards Manali and the Kullu Valley *(see page 99)* do so via the Zanskar region, reachable in 10 to 12 days. From there, you can press on across Shingo La to the roadhead at Darcha in a further 10 days, and pick up buses back to Manali. In winter, Zanskaris imprisoned by snowbound passes are able to reach the outside world only by undertaking a perilous trek along the frozen Zanskar River – a route known as 'Chaddar'.

Most visitors use the town as a base for excursions into the valley, travelling by taxi or local bus to the monasteries (gompas) of **Shey**, **Tikse**, **Stok** and **Likkir**. With a few more days at your disposal, you could consider a longer trip west towards Kashmir, taking in the spectacular Lamayuru gompa and the UNESCO World Heritage monument of **Alchi**, whose architecture, murals and devotional statues date from the first spreading of Buddhism in the 11th and 12th centuries.

The halfway point on the journey to Srinagar (not recommended at present) is traditionally the Shia Muslim town of **Kargil**, where most foreigners turn around and head back to Leh. In 1999, Kargil was the scene of a short but explosive war between the Indian Army and Pakistani-backed militants, who occupied a ridge to the north and started shelling both military and civilian positions in Kargil. The situation is now stable, but anyone planning to travel here should first check that it is safe to do so with the regional tourist office.

Garhwal

The mountain districts to the north of Uttar Pradesh form the region of Uttarakhand and also make up part of the new state of Uttaranchal, which split off from Uttar Pradesh in 2001. Hinduism regards mountains as the dwelling places of gods, and these Himalayas, known as the **Garhwal**, are especially sacred as in them rise the streams that join to form the Ganga and Yamuna rivers. Among the highest peaks is Nanda Devi, rising to 7,817m (25,646ft) and India's highest mountain after Kanchenjunga.

At the base of it all, **Haridwar** is one of the seven most

> In 1968, the Beatles came to Rishikesh seeking spiritual enlightenment at the ashram of Maharishi Mahesh Yogi. Their brief but much publicised visit indelibly fixed transcendental meditation, yoga and gurus in the western consciousness, and Rishikesh has since established its reputation as the yoga capital of the world.

The Laksman Jhula bridge at Rishikesh

sacred cities of India, where the Ganga flows out of the mountains into the plains. Like Allahabad *(see page 87)*, Haridwar hosts a *Kumbha Mela*, a great religious festival, once every 12 years. The evening *aarati* (worship) of the River Ganga is held every day at Har-ki-Pauri, the main ghat.

Rishikesh, a town of temples and ashrams surrounded by forest, is 25km (15 miles) upstream. The northern part of the town, Muni-ki-Reti, is very attractive, and the best views can be seen from either of the two footbridges suspended across the river, the Ram Jhula and the Laksman Jhula.

Dehra Dun lies at the foot of the hills 50km (31 miles) northwest of Hardiwar. It is a fast-expanding town notable for its prestigious institutions, including the Wildlife Institute of India, the Forest Research Institute and the Indian Military Academy, and is also the capital of the new state. On a ridge above Dehra Dun is the hill station of **Mussoorie**, home to the Lal Bahadur Shastri National Academy of Administration, which trains new entrants to the élite Indian Administrative Service, successor to the British colonial Indian Civil Service.

The soaring Bhagirathi Peaks

▶ *Pilgrimage Sites*

Haridwar, Rishikesh and Dehra Dun are the starting points for pilgrimages to the four most sacred places in the Himalayas: Yamunotri, source of the Yamuna; Gangotri, the source of the Ganga; and the temples of Kedarnath and Badrinath.

Yamunotri can be reached from Dehra Dun or Rishikesh. The road stops 13km (8 miles) short of the temple at Hanuman Chatti. From here there is a trek along the riverbank. Pilgrims cook rice and potatoes in the water of a hot spring near the temple and offer them to the goddess Yamunotri.

The road to the pilgrimage site of **Gangotri** runs steeply from Rishikesh via Narendra Nagar, Tehri (where a controversial dam is being built) and Uttarkashi. Gangotri, with Ganga's shrine and cluster of guesthouses that have to cope with some 250,000 pilgrims a year, is situated at 3,140m (10,300ft). From here it's a day's easy trek to **Gaumukh** ('cow's mouth') where the Ganga springs from the base of the **Gangotri Glacier**. Gaumukh is surrounded by some of the most impressive mountain scenery in India, including the 6,543m (21,466ft) **Mt Shivling** (the Phallus of Shiva), which rises as a sheer pyramid above the delightful meadow of **Tapovan**, across the other side of the Gangotri Glacier. This massive 40km- (28 mile-) long river of ice carves its way through the mountains to the northeast, a skyline dominated by the impressively pointed **Bhagirathi Peaks** (6,856m/22,493ft).

The road to Badrinath, home of Lord Vishnu, rises slowly from the steep valley of Deoprayag to the old Garhwal capital of Srinagar. From here the route leads to **Joshimath**, seat of the great Hindu reformer and sage of the 8th century, Adi Shankaracharya. He is credited with establishing the temples at Badrinath and Kedarnath. The Narsingh Bhagwan temple here is the main centre of worship to Vishnu when his shrine at Badrinath is closed during winter. Beyond Joshimath, at Govind Ghat, is the starting point for treks to the **Valley of the Flowers National Park** which is carpeted with flowers during the spring in April and May, and to the modern Sikh temple at **Hemkund**. The road continues up to the Vishnu shrine at **Badrinath**. The shrine at nearby **Kedarnath** is dedicated to Shiva and contains one of the 12 *lingas* (phallic symbols) of light. The temple stands at the head of the Mandakani River, in a stunning valley surrounded by snow-covered mountains.

Corbett National Park

At the foot of the Himalayas, some 300km (180 miles) east-northeast of Delhi and accessible from the capital either by train to Ramnagar (6 hours) or road to Dhikala (8 hours), is the **Corbett National Park**. Among India's nature reserves, this is the best known because of Jim Corbett, the audacious hunter of the man-eating tigers of Kumaon. The park was established in 1935

Take a ride on an elephant at Corbett National Park

A misty Ramganga River as dawn breaks over Corbett Park

and was given Corbett's name after India became independent. The lovely expanse of forest and meadows by the Ramganga River remains a home to the tiger, leopard and elephant, as well as cheetah, sloth bear, wild pig, jackal and hyena. The river abounds with mahseer and trout, as well as two kinds of crocodile and the occasional blind freshwater dolphin. Bird-watchers should look out for stork, red jungle-fowl and black partridge. The forest is thick with sissoo and tall sal trees; their timber is prized for ship-building. An elephant ride, which allows you to swing through the jungle and grassland while reclining on a cushioned howdah, is a great joy. Rest at midday in the lodge at Dhikala and watch the elephants head down to the river.

Be sure to plan ahead through the India Government Tourist Office or a Delhi travel agency because admission to the park is by permit only. However, permits are very easy to obtain and reserved accommodation can be booked either in the lodges or in the official campgrounds. Note that the park remains closed during the monsoon, between mid-June and mid-November.

RAJASTHAN

Rajasthan is one of the most romantic regions in India. Known as Rajputana ('Land of Kings'), and stretching from Delhi to Pakistani Sindh and the Punjab, this is where the Rajput warriors erected their desert and lake palaces. Their fortresses were built with granite or sandstone from the surrounding hills and, in some cases, the same dazzling marble used for the Taj Mahal. Jaipur is the 'pink city', with the famous Palace of the Winds and massive Amber Fort nearby. Further east, Jaisalmer and Jodhpur both developed as trading posts for the ancient caravan routes plying the route from the Indus Valley to the Thar Desert, and Ajmer grew wealthy from the trade between Delhi and Gujarat. In spite of the droughts that have plagued the region in recent times, this is a land of cattle-herders too, and one of their most spectacular sights is the annual market-festival or *mela* at Pushkar held in November.

Probably descendants of the invading Scythians and Huns, the Rajputs were a formidable opposition met by the waves of invaders: Turks, Afghans and Mughals. The Rajputs themselves claimed to have been descended from the Aryan dynasties of the sun and moon. This was accepted by the Brahmin priesthood and they were duly inducted into the Kshatriya warrior caste, to which they continue to proudly belong to this day.

While nearby Malwa and Gujarat came under Muslim rule, most of Rajputana remained Hindu. Towns with the suffix *-pur* had Hindu rulers; *-abad* is the Muslim suffix. Some Rajput princes pursued an independent line. Others sent their daughters to the Mughal harem or their sons to serve as officers in the

Mosaic at the City Palace, Udaipur

Street musician, Amber

imperial army. They enjoyed a privileged position during the British Raj.

Jaipur

Jaipur, the capital of Rajasthan, was constructed according to precepts originally set down in ancient canonical texts on astrology and architecture known as the 'Shastras'. Raja Jai Singh II, that scholar of the stars who dotted northern India with his collections of instruments for observing the heavens, chose an exact date for moving his capital from Amber – 17 November 1727 – as auspicious. He then laid it out according to the disposition of the stars and planets.

Amber Fort

But let's begin at **Amber**, 9km (5½ miles) northeast of Jaipur. Located high on a hill commanding a gorge, the fortress here offered military advantage but was not suited for the kind of development Jai Singh wanted for his capital.

The road up to Amber takes you through classical Rajasthani landscape, its parched hills embracing Lake Maota, where water buffalo snooze lazily in the sun. You may also pass an occasional camel with loaded cart in tow.

The Rajputs of Jai Singh's Kachwaha clan provided visitors to the fortress with an elephant ramp. You can still travel by elephant up through the **Suraj Pol** (Sun Gate) to the **Jaleb Chauk**, a garden courtyard swarming with langur monkeys and surrounded by elephant stables.

A staircase zigzags its way to the Temple of Kali (wife of Shiva), built for the Hindu mother-goddess. The silver doors have bas-relief panels depicting Kali riding various animals. Her statue was brought here from Bengal, where the cult of Kali is particularly strong. The **palace** is a subtle example of the maharajas' opulence: artists banished by Emperor Aurangzeb *(see page 38)* worked on the columns and arches, and on the building's gallery around the **Diwan-i-Am** (Hall of Public Audience).

The Diwan-i-Khas (Private Audience Chamber), known as the **Shish Mahal** (Palace of Mirrors), features the Rajputs' flamboyant taste for covering walls with green, orange and purple glass, and the vaulted ceilings with thousands of little convex mirrors. Strike a match to see the effect.

The most inviting place in the palace is the **Sukh Niwas** (Hall of Pleasure), with doors inlaid in ivory and sandalwood. Inside, cool water was brought down from the roof through a carved white marble chute, and fresh air was brought in through the finely chiselled lattice stonework.

Amber Fort

Jaipur city

The colour of its paintwork has earned Jaipur the name 'pink city', although you will see that it changes colour with both the season and time of day, from a rosy pink to warmest amber, bright orange and dull ochre.

Appropriate for a descendant of the sun dynasty, Jai Singh laid out the city on an axis from the Suraj Pol (Sun Gate) in the east to the Chand Pol (Moon Gate) in the west, a main street that is today a lively bazaar. The town's central focus was the most elaborate Jantar Mantar observatory, which was the final fruit of his labours that had begun in Delhi *(see page 72)*. The initiated will appreciate the significance; to others the mysterious atmosphere of its cream-coloured gnomons (the uprights of sundials), quadrants and sextants will have an esoteric charm.

Chandra Mahal (Moon Palace), directly south of the observatory, is also known as the **City Palace**, with seven interlocking courtyards and stories. A museum inside the building gives an intriguing insight into the life and heyday of the maharajas: their rich costumes, their scimitars and rifles inlaid with bright jewels and silver, and a horrible bludgeon with a double serrated edge.

The textile museum, housed in the **Mubarak Mahal** designed by the British engineer Sir Swinton Jacob, is particularly fascinating. There is an excellent collection of Mughal and Rajput costume, shawls, screens and carpets. Perhaps the prize exhibit is the huge robes of Madho Singh I.

Overlooking the street on the eastern edge of the complex is the **Hawa Mahal**, literally the Palace of the Winds, but actually a rather grand, five-storeyed royal box, in which the women could sit and watch festive processions without being observed. Its airy, projecting oriel-shaped balconies are seen as a symbolic image of Jaipur style. There's a fine view from the top of the zigzag staircase.

Ajmer

Ajmer served as the imperial capital under the Mughal Emperor Jahangir around the turn of the 15th and 16th centuries, and for 2,000 years before that its hillfort – the Taragarh – was the most strategically important in

The Palace of the Winds in Jaipur

all of India. However, the town's historic prominence is these days eclipsed by its significance as the site of Islamic India's most revered shrine: the **Dargah (tomb) of Khwaja Muin-ud-din Chishti**. Visitor numbers, always high, reach their peak at the time of the saint's Urs, or death anniversary, in October/November, when millions from across the subcontinent converge here to pray at the shrine.

Khwaja Muin-ud-din, who originally travelled to Ajmer with other Sufi mystics from Afghanistan in the 12th century, was buried in 1236. His original brick tomb was re-clad in white marble 200 years later by the Mughals, and it was under their patronage that the Dargah became the empire's holiest site. Inside the high-walled compound, through which streams of pilgrims pass daily carrying gold-edged silk and baskets of rose-petal offerings, are interred various minor Mughal royals

Bharatpur and Ranthambore

Situated just 42km (26 miles) due west of Agra on the Jaipur Road, the marshes of the bird sanctuary of **Keoladeo-Ghana** at Bharatpur offer a welcome change of pace. Even if you're not an avid bird-watcher, you'll enjoy the gentle walks in the woodland, with the chance of seeing exciting herds of nilghai antelope, blackbuck and cheetal (spotted deer). A good time to visit is just at the end of the monsoon in October when you can see flocks of storks, egrets and cormorants and it is ideally combined with a full-moon trip to the Taj, but there's plenty to see all year round. Among over 300 different species of birds here, there are eagles, cranes, pelicans, kingfishers and a host of ducks and geese.

Located in southeast Rajasthan, **Ranthambore National Park** is home to around 30 tigers, as well as cheetal, nilghai, jackals, panthers and many birds. Once a royal hunting ground, the park contains several ruined palaces and pavilions. The best time to visit is in the dry season (October to April), when animals venture out of the bush to find water.

and dignitaries. The shrines are tended by fair-skinned hereditary priests called Khadims, who claim descent from Ajmer's
first Sufi missionaries. The hour just before sunset on Friday,
is the best time to be here, when *Qawwali* musicians serenade
Khwaja Muin-ud-din's tomb.

Other Islamic monuments worth hunting out in Ajmer include
the **Adhai-din-ka-Jhonpra Masjid**, 5 minutes' walk north of
the Dargah. The mosque's facade, dating from 1153, bears some
exquisitely carved Qu'ranic calligraphy and is regarded as one of
the finest examples of Muslim architecture in India. Across town,
the Magazine is a fort where Jahangir used to hold court. It was
here, in 1615, that Ambassador Sir Thomas Roe was received
by the emperor – one of the
first encounters between the
Mughals and the British. The
meeting would eventually
bear historic fruit in the form
of a trade agreement allowing
East India Company ships access to Mughal ports – in effect the start of the process
that would, ultimately, become British India.

**Mother and child at the
Pushkar Fair**

With a few hours to spare,
you might also consider the
memorable walk up to the
Taragarh Fort, which lords
over Ajmer from atop a sheer
escarpment. This was originally a Hindu Rajput stronghold but now holds several
Muslim tombs – essential
stops on the Dargah pilgrims'
trail. The views from its ramparts over the plains and city
below are stupendous.

Pushkar, on its desert lake

Pushkar

▶ Hindu mythology identifies **Pushkar**, just across the hills from Ajmer, as the spot where a lotus flower dropped by Brahma, the Creator, fell to earth. A gorgeous little lake promptly sprang out of the Thar Desert, regarded by Hindus as one of India's most sacred sites. During the full moon of Kartika month (early November), tens of thousands come to bathe in the redemptive waters, and to buy and sell livestock at the huge **Camel Mela** held in the dunes to the south of town. The fair has become a major tourist event, for which a whole town of tents is set up.

Even if your visit doesn't coincide with the famous *mela*, Pushkar deserves a detour. Set against a backdrop of sharp-ridged hills – the **Nag Pahar**, or 'Snake Mountain' – the lake and its entourage of domed temples, bathing ghats and white-washed *havelis* (merchants' houses) forms one of Rajasthan's defining sights. For the ultimate panoramic view, climb up the flight of ancient stone steps to the **Savitri Temple**, southwest of town, from whose terrace you can look down the Aravalli mountain range and across the Thar, rippling into the distance.

Jodhpur

Of all Rajasthan's citadels, Jodhpur's **Meherangarh Fort**, perched high on its sheer cliffs at the eastern edge of the Thar Desert, must surely rank among the most imposing. The Rathor Rajputs, always a belligerent bunch and bad trouble for Mughal foes and the Rajputs, built it in the 15th century. Akbar decided it was better to have them on his side than to try to convert them; when he married the Maharaja of Jodhpur's sister, Jodha Bhai (for whom he built a grand palace at Fatehpur Sikri; *see page 84*), there was no question of converting her to Islam.

Near the east gate, you'll see tombstones where soldiers died defending the fort, and cannonball scars indicating efforts by the Maharaja of Jaipur to snatch a promised bride, Princess Krishna Kumari, against her will; she took her own life during the battle. On top of the ramparts the fort displays its proudest possessions: a set of fierce-looking howitzers and a few cannons. From here there is a fine view of the famous blue-and-whitewashed city. The blue colour is popularly said to denote homes belonging to the Brahmins, or priestly, caste, but it was probably a means of protecting property from attack by termites, being made of insect-proof copper sulphate.

Behind the ramparts and the gates with sharp iron spikes to stop elephants from ramming them, there is a very handsome residential palace. Its majesty is most notable in the balconies of the **Royal Harem**, which have screens (*jalis*) of the most delicate pierced stone latticework. The palace **museum** displays a colourful collection of exhibits, giving insight into the daily life of those who lived there. There are luxuriously

Rajput princes attached great importance to titles. At first they were known as Rao or Rana ('Chief' or 'Chieftain') of their clan. Akbar made them happy by calling them Raja ('King'). From there, they promoted themselves to Maharaja ('Great King') or, higher ranking, Maharana, then Maharaja Dhiraj ('Great King of Kings').

Jodhpur – a patchwork in blue

embroidered elephant howdahs, as well as babies' cradles and ladies' palanquins. A version of a sedan-chair, a palanquin was either completely closed up so that a promised bride was invisible while inside, or constructed with a peep hole to allow her to see out – and be seen – when she was married.

At the **Iron Gate** exit, you'll see a more poignant side of the life of a maharaja's wife – 15 scarlet *sati* handprints on the wall, from widows who threw themselves onto their husbands' funeral pyres in ritual sacrifice, in keeping with the tradition of the era.

In the bustling old centre of Jodhpur itself, you can't and shouldn't miss the **Saddar Market** situated by the old clock-tower. In the stalls around it, spices and grain are piled up in multicoloured mountains; merchants chant as they measure out separate lots of 5kg (11lb) each: 'three, three, three', 'four, four, four', and 'five, five, five'. The fort always looms on the horizon, a constant reminder of the town's war-torn history.

Just 9km (5 miles) due north of Jodhpur, the maharajas' mausoleum is in a pretty park on the site of the old capital of **Mandor**, where a number of temple-like memorials, or *chattris*, are built on the site of the maharajas' funeral pyres. The other attraction here is the so-called **Hall of Heroes** – ranks of life-sized carvings of warriors and gods hewn from the rock face.

If you're going to Jaisalmer by road, it's well worth a detour to **Osian** to see the stunning Hindu and Jain temples, many of them dating as far back as the 8th century. Somehow this ancient sculpted pantheon of Hindu deities and Jain prophets has survived the sometimes ferocious weather of India and the iconoclasts of Mahmud of Ghazni.

Jaisalmer

The sandstone citadel of **Jaisalmer**, protected by an imposing double set of bastions, rises like a mirage from the sands of the Thar Desert. Until the late 19th century, it lay on one of Asia's most prosperous trade routes, connecting China, Tibet and the Gangetic plains with the ports of Gujarat and Sindh. But the coming of the railways heralded its demise, which was sealed when Partition created a closed border to the west in 1947.

Jaisalmer, founded by the Maharawals in 1156, is the oldest of Rajasthan's fortified cities. Though much of the city has grown up outside the fort – modern in time, but not in style – 3,000 people live within its walls. Some of their houses in the side streets are from the 12th century. The best views of the citadel are to be had from the rooftops of its ornately carved *havelis*, many of which these days accommodate atmospheric hotels.

The elaborate sculpture in four 15th-century **Jain temples** within the fort finds its counterpart in the finely carved facades of the merchants' havelis, built 200 years later, and sheltered from

Jaisalmer domes

sandstorms on the northeast side. But much more than the individual monuments – handsome but hardly grandiose, because of the restricted spaces available – it is the general atmosphere of the town that gives it its special magic. Everything here is bathed in a serene desert light that adds a shimmer to the stone and a translucence to the shadows.

➤ To see the **desert** at its best, go out at dawn and at sunset. Beyond Jaisalmer, you'll find the road peters out at the village of **Sam**, where streams of tourists, hawkers, guides, camel-ride wallahs and sundry hangers-on gather at sunset to enjoy the largest expanse of dunes accessible by road. Nearby, Indian military installations remind you of the proximity of the fractious Pakistan border. On the way to the village you'll come across a 'camel-station', from where you may wish to take a ride. For fans of this quaint form of transport, longer camel safaris can be set up through Jaisalmer travel agencies. Ask the camel driver to direct you to the still uncharted village of **Kuldhara** – uncharted

Making tea in the desert near Khuri

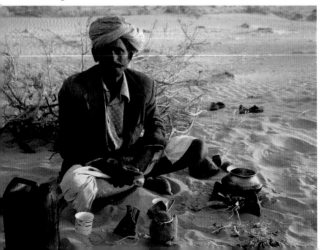

because it was one of 84 villages abandoned over 160 years ago by the clan of Paliwal Brahmins, who, after living there for centuries, left suddenly during the night, rather than having to face paying the new, arbitrary land tax. It still stands as a ghost town – groups of dilapidated square houses made from sandstone.

Out in the desert just 40km (25 miles) southwest of Jaisalmer, lies the village of **Khuri**. The main attraction here is the desert solitude and beautifully decorated houses of mud and straw. Accommodation options are also available to get an authentic flavour of desert life, and camels can be hired locally.

Bikaner

Away to the northeast, **Bikaner** was founded in 1488. Rao Bika, a son of the ruler of Jodhpur, was given an army and asked to seek his own fortune to avoid a war of succession. Thus Bikaner sprang up in the heart of the wilderness called Jangaldesh. Perhaps the very bareness of the landscape spurred the human hand to create beauty. The red sandstone carvings at the **Lalbagh Palace** and those in marble are delicate. **Junagarh Fort**, built in the 15th century, was never conquered and contains palaces and temples of great refinement. Bikaner's art of miniature painting is highly rated; the **Durbar Hall** has breathtaking frescoes, gilded stucco mouldings, floral patterns and incredibly delicate carpets. The **Old Town** has a number of lovely havelis, the finest of which lie along Rampuria Street and Purana Bazaar.

The rugged countryside around Bikaner is dotted with intricately carved 16th-century Jain temples. **Deshnok village**, 30km (16 miles) south, is visited by huge numbers of Hindus as the site of the famous **Karni Mata Temple**. The shrine's presiding deity is an image of a 14th-century female bard, or *charani*, who rose to become a powerful local cult leader and patron goddess of the royal family. What really distinguishes the temple from all others in India, however, is that members of Karni Mata's family are believed to be reincarnated here as rats *(kaba)*. Tens of the thousands of the holy rodents scamper free through the marble precinct, where they're fed by adoring worshippers.

North of Bikaner, between Suratgarh and Anupgarh, is the Harappan site of **Kalibangan**, dating back to around 3000BC. The two largest sites, Moenjo Daro and Harappa, are now in Pakistan, but Kalibangan, a citadel on the banks of the Ghaggar River, is the third city. The excavation and finds show, as at all Harappan sites, a high degree of social organisation, with a well-designed sewage system and a uniform system of weights and measures.

Udaipur

If Jaisalmer is the city of the desert, then **Udaipur** is its opposite: the city of lakes and gardens. The lakes were created by the Maharana Udai Singh for his new capital by damming up the Berach River after Akbar had ransacked his mountain redoubt at Chittorgarh.

Udaipur

Lake Pichola, 4km (2½ miles) long and 3km (2 miles) wide, is the largest lake. Cruises are available from the Bhansi Ghat, which is near the City Palace. This will enable you to travel out to the **Lake Palace Hotel**, even if you're not staying there. The southern end of Pichola has the best view of the lake, taking in the two island-palaces and the City Palace beyond.

The 16th-century **City Palace** on the east shore of the lake is now part royal residence, part luxury hotel and part museum. The sun symbol of the maharana is everywhere. The armour displayed includes an outfit for disguising horses as elephants. The frescoes illustrate the tragic story of Princess Krishna's suicide at Jodhpur; glass baubles, some as big as golf balls, have replaced real jewels in the mosaics.

Most of the interest in Udaipur city centres on its old quarter, packed behind the ghats on the eastern shores of the lake. Competing for the best views, several fine havelis still stand on the waterside, including the enormous **Bagore-ki-Haveli**, a former prime minister's residence converted into an engaging museum, where live performances of Rajasthani folk music and dance are staged several times weekly. Up the hill towards the City Palace is the elaborately carved **Jagdish Temple**, home to a black-stone Vishnu in his incarnation as Jagannath.

For recitals of Rajasthani music and dance, and displays of regional handicrafts, jump in a taxi to the wonderful Shilpagram complex on the outskirts of Udaipur. Among its permanent exhibits are authentically constructed replicas of traditional dwellings, made by tribal minorities and castes from remote corners of Rajasthan and Gujarat.

A pleasant drive along the banks of Fateh Sagar – the second, and larger of Udaipur's lakes – takes you 5km west of the city towards Rana Sajjan Singh's late-19th century **Monsoon Palace**, or Sajjan Garh. From its eerie atop a steep-sided mountain summit, this once beautiful hunting lodge surveys a vast sweep of the Aravallis.

Around Udaipur

Although Udaipur lies within a spur of the Aravalli Hills, the watershed of the range rises 80–100km further north. Crowning one of it most dramatic peaks, **Kumbalgarh Fort**, 84km (52 miles) north of the city, served as an important stronghold for the Ranas of Mewar, who would flee here in times of war. Encircled by a vast loop of crenellated ramparts that, in places, resemble the Great Wall of China, the 15th-century fort makes a

Surveying the scene from Chittorgarh citadel

perfect destination for a long daytrip or two-day excursion, not least because of the idyllic countryside you have to cross the reach it. At the citadel's highest point sits the palace to which the young Rana Udai Singh, heir to the Mewar throne, was spirited away to by his wet nurse during the Mughal siege of Chittorgarh in 1535. The views from its arched windows across the plains of Rajasthan are extraordinary.

Down the mountain from Kumbalgarh, separated by a tract of dense forest where Bhil tribal people still hunt with bows and arrows, stands one of India's largest complexes of Jain shrines. Built of creamy white marble, the temples of **Ranakpur** are as elaborately carved as those at Dilwara, in Mount Abu *(see page 128)*, though they see barely a trickle of foreign visitors.

En route to Kumbalgarh and Ranakpur, it's worth stopping at **Eklingji**, where the Rana of Mewar's protective deity resides in a grand white-marble shrine 22km (14 miles) north of the city, and at the popular **Nathdwara Temple** – one of the state's principal Hindu pilgrimage sites. The latter, 48km (30 miles) north, was established during the 17th-century reign of Aurangzeb, when Krishna worship was punishable with summary execution. Priests from Mathura, the blue-skinned god's birthplace, smuggled their beloved deity to this remote spot in the Aravallis to escape Mughal persecution. The site is nowadays a bustling religious enclave, famous for its distinctive *pichwai* paintings depicting scenes from the Krishna story.

Chittorgarh

Chittorgarh, 112km (70 miles) to the northeast of Udaipur and accessible by road or rail, has one of the region's mightiest citadels. Perched on a hilltop that rises sharply from the plains below, the citadel is celebrated for its tales of Rajput heroism. It was attacked three times by a stronger enemy. In 1303, Sultan Ala-ud-Din of Delhi laid siege to Chittorgarh, it is said, to win for himself the Princess Padmini, whose beauty he had been allowed only a glimpse of in a mirror. Rather than submit, the Rajputs' wives and daughters committed *jauhar*, mass self-immolation, while the warriors rode out of the fort in the saffron robes traditionally worn for the last battle unto death. Over 200 years later came another heroic resistance against the Sultan of Gujarat, ending in another tragic *jauhar*, in which 13,000 women are said to have died along with 32,000 saffron-clad Rajputs. The last stand came with the devastating attack by Akbar in 1567, and one final suicidal sacrifice and battle.

Entering the northwestern side, you can go through seven gateways to see the remains of the Rajputs' heroic exploits: stones mark where each of these brave soldiers fell in battle. South of the Main Gate, the 15th-century **Palace of Kumbha** is built over the cave where Padmini led the first *jauhar* and to which the Rajputs' descendants return for an annual celebration. Some of the walls in the palace were built with pieces of stone removed from Buddhist temples. Kumbha's **Jaya Stambha** (Tower of Victory), 37m (120ft) high, was built by Maharaja Rana Kumbha to celebrate his great victory over Sultan Mahmud Khalji of Malwa in 1440. The tower's nine stories are decorated with Hindu deities, but otherwise it seems inspired by the Kirti

Stambha, an earlier Jain Tower of Fame, built in the 12th century. At the southern end of the site, beside a pond with a pavilion in the middle, is **Padmini's Palace**, where the princess is said to have passed her last days. It is unlikely that the mirror in the room overlooking the pond was the very one in which the sultan got his fatal peek at her, but the guides like to tell the story this way.

Chittorgarh itself, with a population of 100,000, is spread along the banks of the River Ghambiri, surrounded by fertile plateauland where opium cultivation dominates the local economy.

Mount Abu

One of the great sights of India, the **Dilwara Jain Temples** are located on **Mount Abu**, which was developed by the British as a hill station (now used by middle-class Indians). The best way to get here is by train from Jaipur or Ahmadabad.

Dilwara Temple, Mount Abu

According to Jain tradition, Mahavira, the last of the 24 Tirthankara, spent a year here. Of the five main temples, Adinath and Neminath display the finest carving in white marble. Adinath, the most celebrated, was built in 1031 and is dedicated to the first Tirthankar. The lotus ceiling in the main shrine is carved from a single block of marble. Neminath was erected in 1230 to celebrate the 22nd Tirthankar, and the Hall of Donors is particularly fine. The 24 élite Chauhan clans of Rajasthan claim descent from the holy fire that springs from the peak of Mount Abu.

THE WEST

This section takes in the states of Maharashtra, Madhya Pradesh, Gujarat and Goa. As well as bustling Mumbai and stunning Goan beaches, highlights include the spectacular cave temples at Ajanta and Ellora, the stupas of Sanchi and the temples of Khajuraho; there are further cultural treasures in Bhopal, and northern Madhya Pradesh has the twin jewels of Gwalior fort and the medieval city of Orcha. It's possible to see tigers at the wildlife sanctuary of Kanha, while Asiatic lions still roam the Gir Forest in Gujarat.

Mumbai (Bombay)

'Gateway of India' still describes the main function of Mumbai, known until 1995 as Bombay. For those who want to work their way down to the south, Mumbai is still, as it was for the servants and soldiers of the British empire, the natural starting point.

Rather than Delhi, Mumbai is the place for Raj buffs to start out, for it holds some of the most splendid and best preserved British-era buildings in India. Once just a chain of swampy, malaria-ridden islands inhabited by a few fishermen and peasants tapping toddy from the palm trees, it didn't seem a great loss to the Sultan of Gujarat when he ceded it to the Portuguese in 1534. They passed it on to the British as part of Catherine of Braganza's dowry to King Charles II in 1661. The East India Company picked it up for a song at a rent of £10 a year for the next 62 years.

After years of intimidation by the Portuguese, the Hindu, Parsi and Jewish merchants now flocked into the burgeoning port. The island-swamps were drained and linked together by landfills to form one Bombay Island, separated from the mainland by the easily bridged Thana Creek. Modern docks were constructed, and the first cotton mills were completed in 1853, followed quickly by other factories to install Bombay's own industrial revolution. Militarily, Bombay was British India's naval centre and, as you will see from the many warships in the harbour, remains today the headquarters of the Indian Navy.

An occasional luxury liner still glides past the great stone triumphal arch, the harbour promenade of Apollo Bunder, and the Yacht Club to dock at Ballard Pier. For the rest of us landing at CST Airport, the old turmoil of dockside porters and rickshaws that once submerged the newcomer has been replaced by a more modern kind of bustle. With new skyscrapers shooting up almost every month, Mumbai is the busiest industrial and commercial centre in India – cars, textiles, chemicals, nuclear energy and shipping – and a focus for the cinema and the renewal of Indian art. But this huge wealth is juxtaposed with abject poverty, epitomised by women carrying bricks on their heads to build luxury apartments, and by the existence on the city's outskirts of Asia's largest slums.

For anyone who is not here on business, three days, at most four, should be enough to get a good idea of this exhausting city. If you need some initial help getting your bearings before exploring the sprawl that stretches in a wide crescent over 20km (12 miles) from north to south, go to the **India Government Tourist Office**, situated opposite Churchgate Station. Then begin just where King George V and Queen Mary did on their visit back in 1911, on the promontory at the end of Apollo Bunder. This site is marked today by the world-famous **Gateway of India**, a monument moving for its symbolism more than its beauty (depending on how you feel about the pomp of the British empire it was built to celebrate). Rudyard Kipling insisted in his *Ballad of East and West* that 'never the twain shall meet', but the British have done their best, perching four Gujarati domes on this otherwise very Roman concept of a triumphal arch. This edifice was inaugurated in the year 1924; the Somerset Light Infantry solemnly marched through it to their ships some 24 years later – the last British troops to leave India.

The Indian equestrian **statue of Shivaji** faces the gateway. It was erected in 1961 to

The bard of the Raj, Rudyard Kipling, son of the local art school teacher, was born in Bombay in 1865.

The Gateway of India

honour the Maratha hero of Hindu nationalism who fought against the Mughals *(see page 39)*. Beside him is the **Taj Mahal Hotel**, built by a member of the Tatas, a Parsi industrialist family, allegedly when the best hotel in the city at the time, Watson's, refused him entry. Architecturally, it is also a mixture of Western and oriental styles, and a surviving part of the traditional tour that took world travellers from the West to Shepheard's in Cairo, Raffles in Singapore, the Peninsula in Hong Kong and the Imperial in Tokyo. You can get a whiff of the old romance by taking tea in the Sea Lounge and enjoying the harbour view.

The Raj District

Northwest from the Taj, in the area around the Maidan that was the heart of British Mumbai, connoisseurs can appreciate the architecture that fans call 'eclectic' and foes 'mongrel'.

The old Secretariat is mostly described as Venetian Gothic, the University Library French Gothic, the Telegraph Office Romanesque, and the High Court and the Cathedral of St Thomas as Early English. The architects were British but the artisans were

Open-air laundry at Mumbai

Indian – and adept at adding detail reminiscent of Rajput forts and Mughal palaces.

The national mood is stressed on the octagonal spire of the university's **Rajabai Clocktower**, with 24 figures representing the castes of the former Bombay Presidency, of which the city was the capital. Even the most anti-imperialist may be touched in **St Thomas' Cathedral**, by some of the poignant epitaphs for those who died in the military or civil service for their country. For big Raj-buffs, the supreme example of Indo-Gothic style is the **Victoria Terminus**, abbreviated to VT and now CST (Chhatrapati Shivaji Terminus). Inaugurated on Jubilee Day 1857, it served both as a gateway for India's first railway and as a symbol for all that the British had thus far achieved in the subcontinent; of its pride, power and seemingly boundless potential.

Northwest of CST is the bustling **Crawford Market** (known in post-Independence as Mahatma Jyotiba Phule). Behind the brick facade with bas-relief friezes by Kipling's father over the gate, the stalls retain their original layout: vegetables to the left; fruit and flowers to the right; and fish, mutton and poultry straight ahead.

Uptown

Beyond Crawford Market lies the heart of Mumbai, where Indians from the entire subcontinent compete with lively Maharashtrans in the **bazaars**. Among the extravagantly coloured Hindu temples, and mosques in the Muslim neighbourhoods, Jain merchants sell gold in the Zaveri Bazaar, while other streets specialise in silver, brass, copper, leather and lace.

Another famous landmark in the city is the promenade of **Marine Drive**, around Back Bay from Nariman Point to the residential area of Malabar Hill. One must-see is **Chowpatty Beach**, not for swimming or sunbathing, but because it is one of the greatest people-watching spots in western India: fakirs and fakers walk on fire, sleep on nails, climb ropes in midair, or bury their heads in the sand; food vendors hawk kulfi ice cream as well as pan, betel and bhelpuri, a spicy local speciality.

Museums

The **Chatrapati Shivaji Museum** (formerly Prince of Wales Museum), at the southern end of Mahatma Gandhi Road, was built in 1871, incorporating elements of medieval Gujarati architecture with those of Bijapur and municipal Manchester. It houses a collection of miniatures and important 7th-century sculptures from the Elephanta caves. The adjacent **Jahangir Art Gallery** illustrates trends in contemporary Indian painting.

Marine Drive

Elephanta

The 7th-century cave-temples of Elephanta Island make a pleasant boat excursion by ferry from the Apollo Bunder. Known as Gharapuri, Sacred City of the Kings, the island was named Elephanta by Portuguese sailors. Although their musket practice damaged many sculptures of Hindu gods in the caves, enough survive to make it a worthwhile stop. Carved out of the sides of a rocky hill at the centre of the island, the caves contain some of ancient India's finest sculpture, including the iconic *Trimurti*, a triple-headed Shiva whose imposing profile has become almost as recognisable to Indians as that of the Taj Mahal.

Also known as 'Maheshmurti', the panel occupies the rear wall of the largest excavation in the complex, Cave 1. Although

The Elephanta caves

some debate surrounds the date this extraordinary relief was carved, scholars are united in regarding it as the high watermark of Hindu plastic art: no other historic statue in the subcontinent emanates such as vivid sense of power and serenity. Flanking it are more splendid bas reliefs depicting mythological scenes, while the main entrance is presided over by a terrifying, multi-limbed guardian deity (*dvarapala*).

Pune

Pune, 170km (105 miles) from Mumbai, was once the capital of the Maratha empire. The British captured Pune at the Battle of Koregaon in 1818 and built an army cantonment alongside the old city. Among the city's attractions are the **Raja Kelkar Museum**, which focuses on traditional Indian arts; the 19th-century **Agha Khan Palace**, which once served as a prison for Mahatma Gandhi and his wife Kasturba (who died here); and the 8th-century rock-cut **Temple of Patalesvar**, carved from a single boulder of awe-inspiring size.

The northern suburb of Koregaon is also famous as the site of the **ashram** of the now deceased guru, Bhagwan Rajneesh, known to his followers as 'Osho'.

Ajanta and Ellora

The cave temples hewn from the granite of the Vindhya mountains in the northwest of Deccan are among the great wonders of India. The elaborate temples and monasteries, carved with simple tools, are superb works of art in themselves; the sensuous painting and exquisite sculpture they contain make them masterpieces.

Both temples are within easy reach of the town of **Aurangabad**. Try not to visit both sites on the same day as they both deserve to have time taken over them. If you are interested in following the historical evolution of the temples, stop off at Ajanta first, where some caves date from the 2nd century BC. Reserve Ellora for a tour during the afternoon, when the caves will be illuminated by sunlight. Reliable official guides from the office of the Archaeological Survey of India offer their services free of charge.

Ajanta

Dating back to the 3rd century BC, the early caves were the work of a regional dynasty. Having remained untouched for 1,000 years, until British soldiers discovered it during a tiger hunt in 1819, **Ajanta** has the advantage over Ellora, whose caves were in constant use as dwelling places.

Early excavations took the form of long apsed chambers centred on monolithic stupas, called *chaityas*. However, by the 4th century AD the old Hinayana (Lesser Vehicle) school of Buddhism had given way to the more exhuberant Mayayana (Great Vehicle) school, which replaced chaityas with more lavishly dec-

Sensuous cave painting at Ajanta

orated *viharas*. The monks both lived and worshipped in these grander halls, embellishing their walls with figurative representations of the Buddha and associated myths rather than with abstract symbols as their predecessors had done.

Of the 29 caves, all of them Buddhist, five are chaitya temples and the rest vihara monasteries. They are cut from a horseshoe-shaped cliff standing 75m (252ft) high above a narrow gorge, which has a small stream running through it. Originally, each vihara had its own stairway down to the stream. The caves have been numbered from 1 to 29, west to east. Experiencing just nine of them will give an impression of the whole. Start in the middle, at the oldest, then work your way east before returning to the historically later caves at the western entrance.

Cave 10 is the oldest of the chaitya temples, dated at about 150BC. Its nave and aisles are divided by 39 octagonal pillars leading to a stupa, with an apse beyond, permitting the circumambulation (clockwise movement of pilgrims around a shrine). There is no representation of the Buddha in this early era.

Cave 9, a sanctuary from the 1st century BC, is smaller than Cave 10. It is dominated by the stupa. The two-storey facade with arched window and Buddha figures in side niches was probably added in the 6th century AD.

Two elephants in a kneeling position welcome you to **Cave 16**, one of the most important of the later caves, created between 475 and 600AD. The Mahayana school encouraged worship of a

Buddha image, which is why the stupa was replaced with a sculpture of Buddha sitting in a posture used traditionally for teaching. Look for the figures of amorous couples on the ceiling.

With the richness and vigour of its mural paintings, **Cave 17** represents the zenith of Ajanta's artistry. The walls, from the 5th century AD, show the 12 stories of Buddha's Enlightenment. Buddha's steadfast resistance to temptation gave the painters of that time a splendid pretext to show the sensual side of court life as a foil to the Master's spirituality. We see him taming an enraged elephant or appearing as the warrior Simhala attacking the Island of Ogresses, while his wife Rani, holding a mirror, languorously prepares her toilet with handmaidens holding her cosmetics.

The sculpted Buddha is seen with the wheel, symbolic of his law *(dharma)*, and two deer, referring to the park at Sarnath where he held his first sermon. Look for two smaller figures on the pedestal, one of which is holding a bowl for alms or offerings – they represent the merchants who financed the cave's construction.

The small chaitya of **Cave 19** is notable for the carved facade and Buddha statues in its interior and for the graceful figures relaxing in the side niches at the entrance. Visit **Cave 26** for a riot of architectural bravura – the elaborately ribbed vaulting, finely carved pillars and richly decorated shrine with seated Buddha.

In both **Caves 1** and **2** there are superb murals of bright-eyed deer, peacocks, monkeys and elephants, and also those depicting the opulent life, with Prince Siddhartha riding away on horseback. The masterpieces, though, are in Cave 1: two spiritual Bodhisattvas on the back wall on either side of the antechamber.

Ellora

The caves of **Ellora** are cut out of a whole hillside of basalt rock, and conceived on a much grander scale than Ajanta's. Villagers have relied on them as shelter during monsoons or epidemics, so the murals have disappeared, but the sculpture has survived. Starting where Ajanta left off – some of the Buddhist artists may well have moved over to Ellora – all 34 caves were made between the 7th and 12th centuries. The first 12 are Buddhist, 17 are Hindu and the other five are Jain. They stretch north–south over 3km (2 miles), allowing you the option of climbing behind some of them as well as approaching from the cave entrance. As you can see from unfinished caves such as 14 or 24, the sanctuaries were 'created downwards', scooped out of the cliff from top to bottom.

The most important Buddhist excavation (1–12) is the only chaitya sanctuary here, the 8th-century **Cave 10**. The Buddha seated in the domed stupa is worshipped by Hindu artisans as Visvakarma, carpenter of the gods, so the sanctuary is known as the 'Cave of the Carpenters'.

Cave 12 consists of a vihara dormitory with three stories. Its sensual, feminine sculptures show significant Tantric Hindu influence. You must imagine these as originally painted, in brilliant colours.

Of the Hindu temples (13–29), **Cave 14** is an interesting transition from the Buddhist caves because in the pantheon of Hindu gods, Vishnu sits in a meditative pose, suggesting he was converted from a Buddha. Another two are similar to the Bodhisattvas of Ajanta. The sculpture shows a dynamic Shiva killing demons and playing dice in the Himalayas, a group of boys playing with the sacred bull and mother goddesses with children.

The masterpiece of Ellora is the **Kailasa Temple** of **Cave 16**. With a ground plan the size of the Greek Parthenon and a structure half as tall again, this was the work of the 8th-century Deccan King Krishna I. In the process of shaping the temple

The astonishing Kailasa Temple at Ellora

and its shrines in an area 82m (265ft) long and some 47m (150ft) wide, leaving the back 'wall' of the courtyard 30m (97ft) high, 200,000 tons of rock were cut from the face of the hill. Whatever was saved in hauling the masonry needed to 'erect' such an edifice was more than counter-balanced by the seven generations of craftsmen who completed their carvings from one piece of rock. The sculptors created a panoply of Hindu tradition – legendary heroes and their battles, hunts and weddings.

The result is a Hindu temple on a grand scale which can be easily compared with its inspiration: the temples of Mamallapuram (*see page 177*), built some 50 years before in the southern region. The huge gateway leads to the *mandapa* worship hall, with the tall pyramid of the shrine beyond, the whole structure symbolising the mythical Mount Meru, Himalayan home of the gods. After seeing the sculpted friezes at courtyard level, you can gain yet another perspective of the temple's fine detail from above, by walking along the stone ledge that leads around the top.

After Kailasa, the Jain caves (30–34), excavated between the 8th and 13th centuries, will come as an anticlimax – and this despite the prowess of their sculptors. **Cave 31** tries to emulate the style of the great Hindu temple on a much smaller scale, but the artists here were working on much harder rock and so abandoned their effort. The most interesting of all is the two-storey **Cave 32**, known as Indra Sabha, notable for the upper floor's extravagant carving and the great stone elephant, more rigid than Kailasa's (because of the tougher stone), but somehow more noble.

Sanchi

About one hour north of Bhopal, the stupas of **Sanchi** are the best preserved ancient Buddhist monuments in India, if not the world. The site, from the 3rd century BC when Emperor Asoka ordered stupas containing the Buddha's relics to be built, crowns a 91m (300ft) hill on the Vindhya plateau.

Stupas were originally burial mounds; Buddhists developed them into shrines of plaster-covered stone, inside which are caskets containing relics of Buddha. Crowned by a *chhattra* (umbrella) made of stone, the stupa was erected on a terrace with a fence to enclose the path. The stupas of Sanchi lay in the jungle until they were uncovered by the British in 1818, but delay in their restoration led to their plunder. Three stupas and the temples and monasteries from the 5th to the 12th century AD can still be seen.

The Great Stupa, **Stupa I**, built in the 1st century BC, envelops a smaller mound erected some 200 years earlier. It is surrounded by stone railings; in the terrace railing are four *torana* gates, off north–south and east–west axes, perhaps in order to deceive evil spirits. Formed by square posts with finely sculptured panels, the gates are topped by three architraves (crossbars), one placed above the other with dwarfs or animals.

Stupa I at Sanchi

At the time Stupa I was built, Buddha himself was not represented in human form, but symbolised by the horse on which he rode away from his palace, by the wheel of law, by his footprints, and by the pipal tree under which he found enlightenment.

The rest of humanity is present in the form of his worshippers, dancers and *yaksi* nymphs. Despite the strict asceticism preached through Buddhism, it is clear that the craftsmen employed were given free rein regarding their joyous sensuality.

The smaller **Stupa III**, to the northeast of the Great Stupa, has one torana gate; it was originally built to contain the relics of the two disciples of Buddha. **Stupa II** is down on the western slope of the hill. Its circular balustrade has four L-shaped entrances with a simpler decoration of flora, fauna and Buddha symbols. Historians have noted that the horsemen are using stirrups, the earliest known example of their use in India.

The priceless relics looted from the interior of the stupas are now on display at the British Museum and Victoria and Albert Museum in London, but you can see other antiquities unearthed here at the small **Archaeological Museum** at the foot of the hill.

Khajuraho

Khajuraho

This village is famous for the erotic sculptures of its medieval Hindu temples. The sandstone structures are marvels of harmony, whose true grace lies in their sensuality. A World Heritage site, the **Khajuraho** temples lie in a wonderful rural location, overlooked by the Vindhya Hills.

We have British hunters to thank for uncovering these masterpieces, around 1840, half-buried in earth and hidden by the overgrown jungle. They didn't see the light of day until their excavation in 1923, 600 years after being abandoned during the Muslim conquests.

Khajuraho was capital of the Rajput kingdom of the Chandellas, a clan that brought vigour to love and war, as is clear in the temples they built from the 10th to the 12th centuries. The temples are divided into three groups: western, eastern and southern. The major ones, in the western group, are in a beautifully kept park with paths leading easily from one to the other. To see the sculptures at their best, go in the morning or afternoon, or both, and then go back at night, when the temples are illuminated.

The lovely **Lakshmana** temple, dedicated to Vishnu, is one of the earliest, and the only one in which each of the four corner shrines is preserved. Four *sikhara* domes rise above the entrance porch leading to the *mandapa* hall for worshippers, a larger hall for dancing girls and the inner sanctuary, surrounded by an ambulatory for walking around the image of the deity. The silhouette suggests the Himalayan home of the gods, but this may be more of a Brahmanic interpretation than the conception of the architect. The sculptures portray not only erotic postures, but also the adventures of Krishna: in one he uses all four arms to fend off two wrestlers.

Visvanartha, built in 1002, is more compact and ultimately more harmonious than Lakshmana. Its sculptures include a flute-playing maiden and a small nymph pulling a thorn from her foot.

The most spectacular temple of the western group is **Kandariya-Mahadeva**, with three domes culminating in the great 30m- (98ft) high sikhara, composed of row upon row of 84 other, smaller sikharas. Created at the height of the Chandellas'

Bhopal

The city of Bhopal, state capital of Madhiya Pradesh, was tragically put on the world map in 1984 by the gas leak from a pesticide plant owned by the US multinational Union Carbide, which killed at least 2,000 and affected tens of thousands of others. However, Bhopal is far more than this. Built on seven hills and around three lakes, it is one of the greatest centres of art and culture in the country. The architect Charles Correa designed Bharat Bhavan, a fabulous multi-arts centre; it contains a Museum of Adivasi Art that displays striking exhibits. Also noteworthy are the Archaeological Museum and Birla Museum, with good displays of sculpture. There are also art galleries, theatres and a library.

The city was founded in the 10th century by Raja Bhoj. The Bhojpur Temple, even in its ruined state, speaks of the greatness of this king, as do the remains of the magnificent Tal Lake, which once covered 600 sq km (230 sq miles) and whose destruction in the 15th century by Sultan Hosang Shah of Malwa altered the climate of the region.

power in the mid-11th century, the sculpture inside is the most sophisticated and ingenious: *apsara* dancing girls and *sura-sundari* nymphs coquettishly yawning, scratching, applying their makeup, or playing with monkeys, parakeets or with their cheerful lovers. The Kandariya is the largest of all the Khajuraho temples and adds, with its grand scale, a special exuberance to the life-enhancing spirit of the place.

The eastern group includes three Jain temples. The most important is the 10th-century **Parsvanatha**, built in the classical Hindu sikhara-domed style and incorporating the sculptural themes of the Vishnu temples. While the religion of the Jains prohibits anything too explicit in sexuality, the ambience of Khajuraho is clearly contagious, and there are a lot of voluptuous, full-breasted women here.

Gwalior and Orcha

Established in the 8th century, **Gwalior** is a city dominated by its hilltop fort, one of the most redoubtable in the world. The best preserved section is the Rajput palace of Raja Mansingh at the northern end, built 1486–1516 and retaining much of its original blue tiling. At the southern end of the fort is the wonderful 8th-century Teli-ka-Mandir ('oil man's temple'). The steep road up to the Urwahi Gate passes a series of Jain sculptures dating from the 7th to 15th centuries. The view from the battlements near the ornate pair of 11th-century Sas Bahu temples is breathtaking.

Gwalior was a centre of Indian court music. Tansen, the great musician of the court of Akbar, is buried here. His 16th-century tomb is set in the pleasant grounds of the impressive domed Mughal tomb of Muhammad Gaur, his guru. A music festival is held here each December in his memory.

Gwalior is a good place from which to visit **Orcha**, a beautiful medieval town, which looks today much as it must have in the 16th and 17th centuries when it was built. It was founded by the Bundela king, Rudra Pratap, on the banks of the sparkling Betwa River. The countryside undulates gently and the builders of Orcha dotted the landscape with palace and fortress, temple and cenotaph. The architecture is a synthesis of traditional Hindu, hybrid Indo-Saracenic and ornate Mughal. One of the finest sights is the view of the architecturally stunning *chatris*, or cenotaphs, from across the blue river with green hills in the background.

Kanha

For the sheer abundance of wildlife, **Kanha** is probably the best national park in India and should not be missed. The journey there might be a little long, but it's well worth the effort. You can either fly into Nagpur or, if you're coming from Khajuraho, take a train to Jabalpur and continue by road. However, it's best to reserve your accommodation in forest resthouses in advance.

The best season is February to May, when you'll be able to see plenty of beautiful cheetal (spotted deer), blackbuck, sloth

A tiger in Kanha National Park

bear, gaur or bison (largest of the wild cattle), wild boar, Kanha's unique barasingha ('12-pointer') swamp deer, and also monkeys galore. Enthusiastic bird-watchers might also spot black ibis and the crested serpent-eagle. But the park is most famous for its tigers, and the 'Project Tiger' campaign is battling against huge odds here to protect the king of India's jungles.

Ahmadabad

Founded by Ahmad Shah I on the site of the ancient city of Karnavati in 1411, **Ahmadabad**, the capital of the state of Gujarat, is a bustling textile and commercial city straddling the Sabarmati River. On the Old Town side head for **Manek Chowk**, where jewellery and fabric traders occupy the ground floors of beautiful old havelis with their carved wooden balconies, windows and doorways. Also worth looking out for is the local fusion of Hindu and Muslim architecture, manifest in buildings like **Sidi Saiyad's Masjid** near Relief Road. The city boasts some striking modern architecture as well.

Gujarati girl

Hridey Kunj, Mahatma Gandhi's ashram at Sabarmati, is a set of austere yet beautiful buildings nestling amid mango trees. It was from here that Gandhi experimented in non-violent methods of political struggle. There is a simple museum displaying Gandhi's spectacles, sandals, photographs, spinning wheel and cloth spun by him.

Tour of Gujarat

To the northwest of Ahmad-abad, stretching towards the Pakistan border, is the **Rann of Kutch**. The word *rann* de-rives from the Sanskrit word *irina*, meaning a waste, and this is indeed mostly a waste-land of vast salt flats and baked and blistered earth. In January 2001 the region was hit by an earthquake which registered 7.9 on the Richter scale. The beautiful walled town of **Bhuj**

> Archaeological finds at Lothal near Dhandhuka in Ahmadabad district, Rozadi in Saurashtra, and, most spectacular of all, the ruined city of Dholavira in northeast-ern Kutch, carry the history of Gujarat back to the Harappan Civilisation, created in and around the Indus Valley 5,000 years ago.

was flattened and villages in the surrounding area were devastat-ed. It is estimated that some 25,000 people were killed.

For those who have a special interest in the life of Mahatma Gandhi, a visit to **Porbandar**, his birthplace on the west coast of the **Kathiawar Peninsula**, is a pilgrimage worth planning. It is a quiet coastal town. Gandhi was born here in 1869, in his ancestral home. With its small rooms, trellised windows and carved balconies, the house has an air of peace and tranquillity.

Standing majestically at shore of the Arabian Sea, **Somnath** is one of the 12 most sacred Shiva shrines in India. Ransacked repeatedly by northern invaders and rebuilt successively in gold, silver, wood and finally in stone, it is said to have been built by Soma, the moon god, in penance and worship of the wrathful Lord Shiva. Nearby, a temple marks the spot where Lord Krisna is said to have been accidentally killed by a hunter's arrow.

Sasan Gir Lion Sanctuary, 40km (25 miles) north of Som-nath, is one of the last places in the world where Asiatic lions can be seen in their natural habitat. One of the earliest efforts at conservation began in the Gir Forest, under the auspices of Lord Curzon, who advised the ruling nawab to protect rather than hunt the local lions. Now the Gir Forest is one of the most important game preserves in India, with more than 250 lions.

The Church of Our Lady of the Mount overlooks Old Goa

Goa

Time to relax – and this former Portuguese colony is the perfect place for it. The beaches are superb, offering all the white sands and palm trees you could wish for. The local cuisine makes use of the best seafood in India.

Instead of flying down, many people prefer to take the spectacular Konkan Railway that runs along the coast from Mumbai to the Goan capital city of Panaji (formerly Panjim). You will get a great look at the often dramatic mountains of the Western Ghats running parallel to the coast during your trip.

After Vasco da Gama landed on the Malabar Coast in 1498, the Portuguese invaded the area and seized Goa from the Sultan of Bijapur in 1510. They held the colony for the next 451 years, until finally Nehru launched an attack and drove them out.

Goa was a vital link for Portugal's colonial trade in the Indian Ocean. It also became a prime base for missionary activity, with its succession of devout followers of different Catholic religious orders – the Franciscans, Augustinians, Dominicans and the Jesuits; the latter led by the priest Francis Xavier, who came to Goa in 1542 to teach in a seminary. The traders have now gone, but the missionaries' legacy lives on: 35 percent of the local population is Catholic, and the ancient churches in Old Goa still stand.

Goa covers an area of 3,700 sq km (1,420 sq miles). As well as historical monuments like churches and the typical Goan-style Hindu temples, there's the scenic contrast provided by the coastal lowlands with their paddy fields and orchards and the rugged Western Ghats with their gorges and waterfalls. The spectacular **Dudhsagar Falls** can even be viewed from the main Vasco to Hyderabad railway line as it cuts across the hills.

Panaji (Panjim)

Situated at the mouth of the Mandovi River, the capital **Panaji** (Panjim) is a pleasant, relaxed kind of a place. It is mainly used by tourists as a transport hub, but there are some sights to see, including the **Church of Our Lady of the Immaculate Conception**, whose whitewashed facade dominates the Main Square or Praca de Flores. There's also the interesting colonial district of **Fontainhas**, with leafy squares, narrow lanes, red-tiled roofs, shuttered windows, iron balustrades and villas painted in pastel shades of blue, green and ochre. Look for old shops with Portuguese names, and little cafés and bars where the locals like to hang out.

Old Goa

The 16th- and 17th-century churches to be found in **Old Goa** have been beautifully restored, but you will doubtlessly notice that without the town buildings that used to surround them, they have acquired the strangely melancholic air of old museum-pieces. The town once had a population of 350,000 with some 100 churches. Nowadays the laterite stonework of the ones that remain is repainted cream and white each October to cover the mould that springs up during the monsoon downpours.

Distinguished from others by the harmonious simplicity of its rib-vaulted nave, **St Francis of Assisi** was built in 1661 on the site of an older church of which nothing now remains. The fine arabesque and floral frescoes are the work of local Indian artists who excelled at the themes wholly familiar to them – this in contrast with their efforts to paint portraits of the saints, with whose images they were, despite the hard work of the missionaries, perhaps not as much at home.

The distinctly Jesuit-style facade of **Sé Cathedral**, the single biggest Christian church in India, has a certain elegance to it, despite a loss of symmetry when its north tower collapsed in 1776 after being struck by lightning. The enormous main altar, which is dedicated to St Catherine of Alexandria, shows some scenes from the saint's martyrdom in a series of sumptuously gilded panels.

Sandstone and granite were the materials used to build the baroque church of **Bom Jesus**, famous for its casket containing St Francis Xavier's relics. Located to the right of the altar, the mausoleum was designed in Florence, as a gift from the Grand Duke of Tuscany. Each year on 2 December the remains of the saint become the centre of a mass pilgrimage when Catholics from all over Goa come to pray; they are joined by a significant number of Hindus, who also venerate the shrine.

> **Every ten years (the next time in 2014) the body of St Francis Xavier is carried from the church of Bom Jesus to be exhibited at the cathedral. But not a lot is left. In 1554 a Portuguese lady bit a toe off; another toe fell off and is kept in a separate crystal box; the right hand was donated to the Catholic community in Nagasaki; and other pieces were sent to Rome.**

Hindu Temples

The biggest concentration of **Hindu temples** in Goa is around Ponda to the southeast of Old Goa. Goan temples feature a multistorey lamp-tower, called a *dipastambha*; when lit up, it becomes a column of flames offered to the deity. These pillars of light came to prominence during the 18th-century Maratha Wars against the Mughals and are unique to Goa. Scholars speculate that they could represent transformed and enlightened minarets, as the Marathas battled so fiercely against the Muslims. One of the most spectacular is the **Shri Shantadurga Temple** at Quela, dedicated to the Peaceful Durga – a title the powerful tiger-riding goddess was given when she mediated in a quarrel between these two gods and pacified them. The annual festival is usually held around mid-February, depending on the moon. The Shri Naguesh, Mahalsa and Manguesh temples nearby are also well worth visiting.

Mahalsa Temple

Goa's Beaches

Goa's entire 100km (60-mile) coastline is strung with idyllic **white-sand beaches**. The first foreign travellers to spot their potential were hippies in the 1960s and 1970s, who were attracted as much by the availability of cheap alcohol and the locals' seemingly liberal attitudes to nudity as the palm trees and surf. Since then, the more accessible of the beaches have been developed into fully fledged resorts, fed by a constant turnover of charter tourists arriving by direct flight from northern Europe, Russia and Israel.

Calangute, in north Goa at the centre of a magnificent 11km (7-mile) beach, forms the hub of the region's tourist scene. A cluttered market lined by bars, shops, restaurants, banks and telecom centres, it is these days popular mainly with domestic visitors who travel here by bus on day trips from the capital, Panaji. At the southern limit of the same beach, **Candolim** is a

Anjuna beach

predominantly British package enclave, overlooked by the laterite walls and canon emplacements of the former Portuguese stronghold, Fort Aguada.

The younger charter holidaymakers gravitate to **Baga**, a resort at the opposite (northern) end of Calangute beach, where Tito's nightclub dominates a busy, brightly lit strip. Signs advertising karaoke nights, 'Full English Breakfasts' and 'Happy Hours' jostle for attention with Kashmiri handicraft vendors and restaurants offering authentic Italian cuisine and cocktails. On Saturday evenings, seemingly every taxi in the state turns out for Ingo's Night Market at nearby **Arpora**, where foreigners sell designer wear and stallholders from across the country tout souvenirs.

The night bazaar evolved out of the older-established Anjuna Flea Market, still held on Wednesdays at the next village up the coast and a major tourist attraction showcasing handicrafts and clothes from all over India. **Anjuna** has long been a bastion of a harder-edged, more hedonistic hippy tourism, with its drug-fuelled full-moon parties and techno dance music, which you can sample at the famous Nine Bar in nearby Vagator after the Flea Market.

North of Anjuna, development thins out after the Siolim River, only rearing its head again at **Arambol**, Goa's northernmost village. Beyond the reach of package tourism, this remains essentially a hangout for long-staying 'alternative' visitors. If you've come to India to learn yoga, have Ayurvedic massages or space out on the beach doing t'ai chi, Arambol will be the place for you.

South Goa is on the whole much more sedate than the north, with most visitors corralled inside one or other of the five-star resorts backing **Colva Beach**. Extending for 25km (15½ miles), this stretch remains comparatively uncrowded even in peak season. While the rather rundown resort of Colva soaks up most of the domestic tourist traffic, independent travellers congregate more in neighbouring **Benaulim**, a predominantly Catholic fishing village that has retained plenty of traditional Goan charm. It also offers the best selection of budget guesthouses in the area. For more luxury, head south of Benaulim to the Taj Exotica, the flagship among the rank of glamorous five-star hotels built behind the beach over the past decade.

In the far south of the state, a couple of hours' ride across the Sayadhri hills, **Palolem** is undeniably Goa's most picturesque beach – a gently curving spread of golden sand set against a curtain of coconut palms. Remote and unfrequented until as recently as the early 1990s, it has since become the first-choice destination for backpackers. Thankfully, however, building has been held in check by the local municipality's ban on concrete construction, and accommodation is mainly in the form of eco-friendly palm-leaf 'huts'.

Fresh fruit for sale

THE EAST

This section takes in the eastern states of Bihar, West Bengal and Orissa. It encompasses the ancient Mauryan capital of Patna and the birthplace of Buddhism at Bodh Gaya, the great Hindu temples of Bhubaneshwar and the sacred town of Puri. After the challenge of Kolkata, you can cool off in the tea plantations of Darjeeling or in the mountains of Sikkim.

Kolkata (Calcutta)

When the body of Shiva's wife, Kali, was dismembered after her death, the little toe of her right foot fell onto the bank of the Hooghly River, and that is where the village of Kalikata grew up. Together with the villages of Sutanuti and Govindpur, it was sold to the East India Company in the 1690s to set up the trading centre of Calcutta (Bengali: Kolkata).

It was the Nawab of Bengal's attack on the British settlement in 1756 that brought Robert Clive's reprisal at Plassey and the consolidation of the British presence in India. Calcutta, with its port connection to East Asia and subsequent development of its jute, cotton, silk and tea industries, remained its capital for the next 150 years. However, the Bengalis and Kolkatans in particular were trouble-makers, violently stirred by the growing nationalism. The British found it wise to move the political capital to Delhi in 1911. Since Independence, when Partition cut its jute and other industries off from their natural hinterland in eastern Bengal, the city has suffered many economic difficulties, compounded by a huge influx of refugees from Bangladesh. It remains a hotbed of radical, left-wing politics.

Kolkata's reputation for squalor has so deeply imbedded itself in the world's imagination that it comes as a surprise to find the Kolkatans are proud of their city and its vigorous intellectual culture. Bengalis are irrepressible; perhaps the challenge of coping with daily life in this city of 14 million has sharpened their wit. Survival here is a creative art; it is no accident that Kolkata remained the country's intellectual and cultural capital

Calcutta's Howrah Bridge

long after it relinquished government to Delhi. Kolkata was the home of the writer Rabindranath Tagore, India's first Nobel Prize winner, and of the philosophers Ramakrishna and Vivekananda. Creative people still make their name here. After the establishment-minded press of Delhi, the newspapers in Kolkata seem bright, ebullient and vitriolic; while Mumbai's filmmakers are masters of melodrama, Kolkata's cinema is known for its sensitivity and poetry, producing faithful mirrors of village and city life in the hands of such directors as Satyajit Ray and Mrinal Sen. It is the proper home for the country's best museum, the aptly named Indian Museum.

The West Bank
Even if you're not arriving by train, start your visit at **Howrah Station**. The teeming crowds will douse you in something of a baptism by fire, and you'll soon realise that only a small fraction of them are actually there to take a train. The station is a home for many: its entrance hall and platforms are dormitory and kitchen.

Head next for the restful **Botanical Gardens**, laid out in the 18th century, boasting 35,000 species of flowers and shrubs. The first tea cuttings were brought here from China to found the plantations of Darjeeling *(see page 159)* and Assam. Occupying pride of place is a 200-year-old **banyan tree**, the *Ficus bengalensis*, or strangling fig tree. Some fungus destroyed its central trunk, but it still thrives, its aerial roots combining to give it a circumference of 330m (1,080ft).

The **Howrah Bridge**, itself a national monument, conveys you across the river. This massive steel suspension bridge stages the most magnificent traffic jams; it is a great place at which to gauge the Bengali temperament.

The City

Another park, the **Maidan**, is in the centre of the city. It was landscaped to allow for a clear line of fire from all around **Fort William**, which was rebuilt by Robert Clive on a more easily defended site than its predecessor. Like Britain's Hyde Park, the Maidan attracts ferocious soapbox orators predicting the end of the world, but it is also visited by the most wonderful charlatans peddling medicine and other questionable substances.

On its northern side, the 48-m (157-ft) high **Ochterlony Monument** was built in 1828 in honour of the British general Sir David Ochterlony, whose outflanking of the Gurkas near Kathmandu decided the Anglo-Nepalese War of 1814–15. With its peculiar mix of architectural styles, it is one of many Kolkata landmarks that has not exactly taken on its new name (Shahid Minar). It is the focus of the city's boisterous political rallies.

Kolkata's clean and efficient Metro system operates Mon–Sat 7am–9.15pm, Sun 3–9.15pm. Platform TVs show films while you wait. Avoid peak hours.

Eden Gardens, with pond and pagoda and the Kolkata cricket grounds, are by the river.

The **Victoria Memorial** offers a history of the bygone Raj, Anglo-Renaissance in style with a touch of Mughal influence. Its white marble was brought from the Rajasthani quarries used for building the Taj Mahal. Commissioned by Viceroy Lord Curzon, it was paid for by 'voluntary contributions' from the maharajas and nawabs. More recently, historians of the Raj have reminded us that its construction corresponded precisely with the third and most lethal of a series of devastating famines in which an estimated 20–30 million peasants starved to death.

The Victoria Memorial by night

Running along the eastern edge of the Maidan, the **Chowringhee Road** (Nehru Road) marks the old European neighbourhood whose mansions once won Kolkata the wishful name of 'City of Palaces'. These days it is a busy shopping street with big hotels and cinemas, gigantic film billboards and a roadway that is choked with traffic. Catch up on the Indian avant-garde at the **Academy of Fine Arts** on the southeast corner of the Maidan.

The **Indian Museum**, by Chowringhee Road and Sudder Street, makes an excellent home for art treasures from the ancient Maurya and Gupta eras. The great Buddhist carvings on the railings from the Bharhut stupa (2nd century BC), comparable to those of Sanchi *(see page 140)*, are preserved in the **Bharhut Gallery**. The **Gandhara Room** displays the earliest sculptures representing Buddha in human form (1st century AD).

Dalhousie Square, on the site of the original Fort William north of the Maidan, was once the centre of Britain's imperial bureaucracy. Here, scribblers of the East India Company – *babus* to friend and foe – duplicated everything they could lay their hands on in the Writers' Buildings. It now serves just the government of West Bengal, but with an undiminished number of babus.

It takes a detective to find the original site of the **Black Hole** at the domed General Post Office on the west side of Dalhousie Square, since most Indians aren't interested in helping you. They generally see the incident *(see page 40)* as having been a piece of elaborate British propaganda thought up to justify Clive's retaliation. A plaque marks the spot in an arch at the northeast corner of the post office.

Most of the major British Indian buildings prior to the 20th century were built not by an architect but by a soldier-engineer copying existing plans of buildings back home. The magnificent **Raj Bhavan** (Governor's Residence), due north of the Maidan, replicated famous Kedleston Hall in Derbyshire. The nearby **St John's Church**, Kolkata's first cathedral, is an Indian version of London's St Martin-in-the-Fields; look in the south aisle for John Zoffany's amusing painting of *The Last Supper*. Zoffany used the East India Company men as models, with the painter's sworn enemy, Mr Paull, as Judas. The tomb of Job Charnock, the Company official

Transport options in downtown Kolkata

who founded the city of Calcutta, is in the cemetery.

The **Marble Palace**, a bizarre tribute to Western art and architecture, can be found on tiny Muktaram Babu Street northeast of Dalhousie Square. Built by the wealthy land-owning family of Raja Majendra Mullick Bahadur, this huge Palladian villa-turned-museum has a park and menagerie of exotic birds. It recalls William Randolph Hearst's castle in California, with its imaginative juxtaposition of ancient Roman and Chinese sculpture, fine Venetian glass chandeliers, Sèvres porcelain, old Flemish masters and naughty French erotica. The odd Mullick still hangs around to play Chopin in the ballroom or billiards in the parlour.

> **South of Kolkata lies the Sunderbans, a stretch of impenetrable mangrove forest that is part of the world's largest delta formed by the rivers Ganges, Brahmaputra and Meghna. It is a vast area, covering 4,264 sq km (1,646 sq miles) in India alone, with a larger portion in Bangladesh. 2,585 sq km (998 sq miles) of the Indian Sunderbans forms the largest tiger reserve and national park in India.**

Darjeeling

Before you overdose on the countless temples or even just on the heat of the plains, follow the wise example of the long-gone British of Calcutta and get up into the hills and greenery which lead to the lush cool of the celebrated Darjeeling tea gardens. At 2,185m (7,100ft), you're well placed to take in the splendour of the Himalayas – Mount Kanchenjunga situated in Sikkim *(see page 163)*, and, if you're lucky on a clear day in April and May or in late September and October, Mount Everest itself, up in Nepal.

In 1835, the raja of the then-independent kingdom of Sikkim was pressured into ceding Darjeeling to the British. The Brits believed it would be a healthy place for soldiers and East India Company employees to recover from the ills of the plains, but above all they found the area strategically useful for controlling a pass into much-contested Nepal. With tea from seeds smuggled out of China and an influx of plantation labour from Nepal, the little village of 100 souls grew to a community of 10,000 by 1849. Now Darjeeling is part of West Bengal, but Nepali remains the official language and most residents are of Nepalese and Tibetan origin. Buddhists account for 18 percent of the population.

A major part of the pleasure of Darjeeling is in getting here. Although you're driving along narrow mountain roads, you'll feel much safer than in the plains because everyone takes more care; lorry and bus drivers are clearly subdued by the deep ravines.

But the best way to travel up – at least part of the way, if you're too impatient to take 6 hours for the whole 80km (50 miles) – is by the **Darjeeling Himalayan Railway**, more popularly and humorously known as the 'Toy Train', which starts out

Darjeeling and Kanchenjunga

at Siliguri, not far from Bagdogra. Built in 1881, the tiny train on a 60cm (2ft) track climbs, loops and zigzags through dense forests of sal, Chinese cedar and teak which are alive with jungle birds and mountain streams. Watch for Pagla Jhora, the Mad Torrent, just after Gladstone's Rock (shaped like the statesman's head). Also keep your eyes open for a first view of **Kanchenjunga**, 8,586m (28,168ft) high and the world's third-highest peak after Mount Everest and Pakistan's K2.

The railway builders admitted it might have been safer to dig some tunnels, but they preferred to go 'round the mountain' to allow for a better view of the terraced tea gardens and the valleys plunging down to the Bengal plains. Certainly when you reach the railway's high point, 2,257m (7,407ft) up at **Ghoom**, the view as you hover out on the loop over Darjeeling is breathtaking.

The only relics of the British Raj are the (now) all-Indian, and still very private, Darjeeling Club, and a couple of tea rooms and Edwardian hotels such as the Windamere (with coal-burning fires and hot-water bottles at night). The real British legacy is in the **tea gardens**, which offer a beautiful setting for the town and an insight into tea growing and processing (*see page 162*). Makaibari and Happy Valley are among those open for visitors without obligation to buy.

A drive out to **Tiger Hill** before dawn has long been a popular excursion for Darjeeling visitors wanting to see the famous sun rise over Kanchenjunga. The summit of the hill is 2,590m

(8,515ft) above sea level, and from the observation platform there is a superb view to the northeast as the sun first lights up the twin peaks of the great mountain, and then the flanks. The peak in the distance that appears to be smaller is in fact Mount Everest; the other summit – the one that looks the highest – is that of Makalu, the world's fifth-highest mountain at 8,463m (27,766ft).

For a closer look at the roof of the world, consider a seven-day trek, on foot or pony, to **Sandakhpu** (3,650m/11,700ft). You'll get better views of Kanchenjunga and Everest and pass through forests of chestnut, magnolia and rhododendron. During April and May, the orchids will be in bloom.

Armchair mountaineers invariably enjoy the excellent museum at the **Himalayan Mountaineering Institute** in Darjeeling. It has on display some fascinating memorabilia of Himalayan expeditions, in particular the equipment used by Sherpa Tensing Norgay (here Indianised as Shri Tensingh), when, with Edmund Hillary, he was the first to conquer Everest in 1953.

Darjeeling Tea

The tea planters in Darjeeling are snobs with something to be snobbish about. Their aromatic tea is India's best; in its purest form it is horrendously expensive, but understandably so, when they get an average of 400kg (550lb) per hectare, compared with some 1,340kg (3000lb) down in the plains.

Darjeeling's dainty 'China' tea – as opposed to Assam's coarse, broad-leafed variety – is taken from the top of the bush, just two leaves and a bud, and taken away to the factory where it is then withered and rolled, fermented, dried and graded. Here, planters never use the 'curl, tear and crush' method (CTC for short) – in fact, veteran Darjeeling planters prefer not to even speak of CTC – which is what the tea planters do down in the plains. The quality of Darjeeling's tea grades is reflected in the poetry of their names: Golden Flowery Orange Pekoe, Golden Broken Orange Pekoe, Orange Fannings, and Dust, which is used for tea bags.

Tibetan Buddhist monks, Sikkim

Sikkim

Once again, a great part of the joy of the place is the journey itself, by road to the capital, **Gangtok** (1,768m/5,800ft), in eastern Sikkim through the most spectacular scenery: rivers roaring through gorges, deep valleys outlined by terraced rice paddies, and forested hills. To protect India's border with China and to put an end to the unrest over the Raja's autocratic rule, the region of Sikkim was incorporated into the Indian Union in 1975. The people of Sikkim are mostly made up of Nepalese and Lepchas – the country's original settlers known also as Rongpan, the people of the ravines – and Bhutias from Tibet.

The colourful Tibetan Buddhist monasteries are the most attractive sight in the valleys near Gangtok. The most easily accessible of them is **Rumtek**, built in 1968 after China drove the maroon-robed Tibetan monks of the Karmapa sect into exile. Other, older monasteries from the 18th century, based 150km (92 miles) west of Gangtok at **Pemayangtse** and **Tashiding**, are well worth visiting, but access to them may be restricted at times by the military authorities.

Bhubaneshwar

Down the coast from Kolkata, **Bhubaneshwar**, the capital of the state of Orissa since 1956, is a city of temples. Once there were thousands of Hindu and Jain sanctuaries in and around the town. Some 500, mostly ruins, can still be traced, but only 30 are visitable. Three or four are masterpieces of Hindu architecture.

The oldest temples, dating from the 7th and 8th centuries, are grouped around the sacred 'Ocean Drop' lake of **Bindu Sagar**, the focus for bathing and purification ceremonies before the annual festivals. East of the Bindu Sagar, the 10th-century **Muktesvara** is a rust-coloured stone temple dedicated to Shiva, with a small bathing tank and gracefully arched torana gate. There is great peace and dignity in the temple's proportions; the low curved pyramid on the hall of worship and ribbed sikhara dome over the sanctum repeat the classic silhouette of Orissa temples.

The **Rajarani**, standing on a platform at the end of a pleasant garden, is a more robust structure than that of the Muktesvara,

Carvings on the Muktesvara Temple at Bhubaneshwar

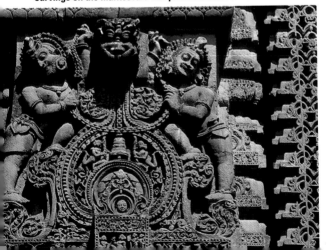

with a more pronounced pyramid over the worship hall, and a powerful sikhara behind it.

The greatest of the city's many temples is the 11th-century **Lingaraja**, south of the Bindu Sagar. Off limits to non-Hindus, it can be viewed from an observation platform specially erected for the purpose by Lord Curzon. A pair of binoculars will be particularly useful here, in order to appreciate the splendid detail of the carving on the soaring central tower dominating a whole complex of temples. It is dedicated to the Lord of the Three Worlds, Tribhuvanesvara, who gave the town of Bhubaneshwar its modern day name.

Udaigiri

Bhubaneshwar is a centre for easy day trips to the ancient Jain cave monasteries of Udaigiri, the chariot-temple of Konark and the sacred pilgrimage town of Puri.

The cave monasteries of **Udaigiri** are close to Bhubaneshwar Airport. Excavated from a sandstone hill in the 3rd and 2nd centuries BC the Udaigiri (Sunrise Hill) caves were dwellings for priests and monks when Jainism was the state religion in the kingdom of Kalinga.

Rani's Monastery (Cave 1) has carvings of elephants, maidens and court dancers, but unlike the caves of Ajanta and Ellora *(see page 135)* there are no temples or central halls for worship.

Further up the hill, **Ganesha Gumpha** (Cave 10) is set back on an esplanade and guarded by two sturdy stone elephants holding branches of mangoes. The friezes are more sophisticated, showing archers riding elephants and a king of Kalinga reclining with his queen. Cave 14, **Hathi Gumpha** (Elephant Cave), is important for the inscription above the entrance, which details the conquests and irrigation projects completed during King Kharavela's 13-year reign, around 50BC.

Konark

The **Sun Temple** of Konark was conceived as a gigantic chariot for the great sun-god Surya cantering seawards to the Bay of

A carved wheel at the Konark Sun Temple

Bengal. The sikhara that once towered 60m (200ft) into the air like some symbolic and divine charioteer has gone, but the grandiose pyramid of the **Jagmohan** (Hall of Audience), where the priests used to officiate, still soars above 12 pairs of huge stone wheels sculpted into its huge platform and drawn by numerous galloping horses. The temple was built in the 13th century, but the sikhara toppled, its porous stone ruined by storms and plunderers and by the ambitious concept of its architect. As you climb over the remains, you'll find they have a decidedly secular air. Surya was given his due with dignified green chlorite statues of *parsva-devatas* (sun-deities) set in niches facing the four points of the compass, and much of the sculpture profusely decorating the walls emphasises his life as a king – his battles, the royal hunt and life at court. The sensuality of the aristocratic lovers recalls Khajuraho *(see page 142)*.

The wheels of the chariot themselves, symbols of the Hindu cycle of rebirth, have beautifully carved spokes and hubs decorated with kings and gods. Beneath the wheels, there are lively carved friezes of elephants playing with children. Look out as well for a giraffe, which indicates the Indian west coast's early contact with Africa. The masterpieces among the free-standing statuary, though, are the war-horses trampling the king's enemies and the splendid elephants crushing the demons.

European sailors, for whom the temple was an important landmark, enabling them to keep out of the dangerous shallows of the Orissa coast (they nearly had it turned into a lighthouse), called it the Black Pagoda in order to be able to distinguish it from the 'White Pagoda' of Puri's whitewashed Jagannath Temple further south. However, after the huge sikhara tower had collapsed the British saved the pyramidal Jagmohan by pouring concrete into its core; now the Archaeological Survey of India is performing massive restoration work on the important sculpture.

Puri

Even if you cannot be in Puri for the tremendous Rath Yatra Festival in June/July, the town is worth a visit just to see a community devoted almost entirely to the 'industry' of its

Wheel of Life

Jagannnath, the Universal Lord, is an incarnation of Vishnu the Preserver, offering Hindus of all castes the opportunity to escape the torment of perpetual rebirth. Thousands of pilgrims congregate at Puri all year round, but mostly for the June/July festival when the three great wooden chariots of Jagannath, his brother and his sister are drawn through the streets. Then, the faithful can liberate themselves by touching the crudely carved wooden deities, models of which are sold in the town.

Although orthodox followers of Vishnu insist that Jagannath is a life-giving force, in previous centuries many sought ultimate release by hurling themselves under the huge wheels of Jagannath's chariot, whence the English word 'juggernaut', which means a great force demanding utter self-sacrifice.

Fishermen at Puri

great **Temple of Jaggannath**, either directly or by trading with the thousands of pilgrims who come here each year.

Non-Hindus are not permitted within the temple precincts, but you can get a good view from the roof of the Raghunandan Library near the temple wall. Some 6,000 priests, artisans and other workers are employed within the grounds. Of the four main buildings, all of them whitewashed and decorated with bright painted sculptures, the first is where the worshippers bring offerings of flowers and fruit, the second is for sacred dances, and the third for viewing the divine effigies, which are enshrined in the sanctum of the fourth and tallest edifice.

Puri also has a beautiful **beach**, southwest of town, which is ideal for cooling off – but those aren't sandcastles the Indians are making, they're miniature temples, for this is the **Swarga Dwara** (Heaven's Gateway), where the faithful wash away their sins. Be sure to watch the *nolia* (fishermen) come ashore through the surf. Although the beach at Puri is one of the best in India, the seas can be very rough, with strong and erratic currents. Caution is advised.

Patna

The capital of Bihar serves as a base for visits to the sanctuaries of Bodh Gaya, Rajgir and Nalanda, but its bazaars, first-class sculpture museum, a major Sikh temple and the views of the Ganga River make it worth at least a day of your time.

Patna was already in existence 2,500 years ago, when Buddha and Mahavira were active here. It later became the capital of the Mauryan emperors, in the 3rd century BC, and one of the largest cities in the world at 3km (2 miles) across and 12km (7 miles) along the Ganga. The British used Patna for manufacturing and distributing opium in the 19th century, to keep China supplied with its favourite drug. The old warehouses can still be seen by the river in the Gulzarbagh district, now housing a printing press.

The **Golghar**, on the west side of town near the river, is evidence of the more altruistic side of British activity in Patna. This great flat-topped dome, a granary some 27m (87ft) high, was erected in 1786 by Captain John Garstin 'for the perpetual prevention of famine', after the terrible famine of 1770. Climb to the top for a fine view of the town and river.

The open ground on the edge of the **Maidan** is where Mahatma Gandhi held mass prayer meetings. Stand in the middle of the new **Ganga Bridge** to get a sense of the effect the river has on the lives of the Indians; it is 3km (2 miles) wide here.

Har Mandir Takht in old Patna will give you a sense of the Sikh community. It was built on the birthplace of Gobind Singh (1666–1708), who called on the Sikhs to defend their faith with armed force *(see page 17)*. The well that served Gobind Singh's house is now a marble shrine. The sanctuary exemplifies piety and militancy. A priest will explain the faith and show you, among the guru's relics, his cradle, shoes and weapons. Above the sanctuary, priests and neophytes chant from the scriptures of the Adi Granth Sahib in a hall, now a museum to history and a record of the tortures suffered by Sikhs. The **bazaar** nearby sells cheap bamboo and leather goods.

Among its many sculptural treasures, **Patna Museum** houses an astonishing collection of Mauryan sculpture. The most famous piece is to the left of the entrance: the *Didarganj Yakshi*, a buff-coloured Mauryan sandstone statue of a woman, remarkable for her brilliant polish, her firm rounded breasts, her navel and her seductive belly and hips. It is considered one of the greatest examples of Indian art of all times.

Bodh Gaya

The site of the pipal tree or bodhi – the tree of wisdom where Gautama Siddhartha became the Enlightened One, Buddha – stands for one of the four great pilgrimages of his life. The others are those of his birth at Lumbini (Nepal); his first sermon at Sarnath (*see page 93*); and of his death at Kushinagar. The sanctuary is just outside Gaya, south of Patna.

E.M. Forster fans can undertake their own private pilgrimage 25km (15 miles) north to the Barabar Caves, which were the setting for the 'Marabar incident' in Forster's famous novel *A Passage to India*. As Forster commented, however, they have no artistic merit in themselves.

The towering structure of the **Mahabodhi Temple**, built in the 6th century, prefigures the gopura gateways of south India.

Waiting for Nirvana

The demons did not make it very easy for Gautama Siddhartha to achieve enlightenment. As he sat there beneath the pipal tree for 49 days, they played the age-old game of 'good guy, bad guy' to distract him. First, they hit him with whirlwind, then tempest, flood and earthquake. He just sat there. Then the devil Mara brought in his lovely daughters, Desire, Pleasure and Passion, to seduce him with song, dance and caresses. He just sat there. They offered to make him king of the world. He just continued to sit until they gave up and went away.

Buddha's ordeal was a godsend for Indian art. In early Buddhism, when it was considered sacrilegious to portray Buddha in human form, his torments and temptations provided sculptors with a rich alternative source to draw upon.

In keeping with other early Buddhist tenets, there is no figurative representation of Buddha here. However, there is a large gilded statue from a later period inside, and behind the temple are the spreading branches and trunks of the sacred **Bodhi Tree**, which is said to have grown from a sapling of the first one that stood here 2,500 years ago. Pilgrims visiting the temple reverently drape its branches with white and saffron-coloured veils. A platform marks Buddha's seat and a set of large footprints symbolise his presence, while stone bowls mark where he walked. Hindus and Buddhists still bathe where he bathed. The museum has stupa railings, and the granite Buddhas date from the 9th century.

Bodh Gaya

The importance of the Bodh Gaya pilgrimage is evident in the Japanese, Thai, Tibetan, Burmese and Chinese temples nearby.

Rajgir

This ancient city is due northeast of Bodh Gaya, out on the road to Nalanda, and it has been holy to both the Buddhists and Jains since the 6th century BC. As Rajagriha, the capital of the Magadha kingdom, the town was frequented at different times by both Buddha and his contemporary Vardhamana Mahavira, the founder of the Jain religion.

The surrounding green hills are topped by numerous temples of both religions, the best known being on Gridhakuta (Vulture's Peak), where Buddha is believed to have converted the once fierce Mauryan warrior king Bimbisara to the peaceful doctrine of non-violence. The Japanese have built a great white stupa on Rajgir's principle hill, which you can reach by aerial ropeway – a pleasant way to survey the rugged countryside.

Nalanda

In order for you to get the most out of the fascinating ruins of the great monastery and the University of Nalanda, it is recommended that you use the services of a guide from the Archaeological Survey of India.

In the 3rd century BC, Asoka founded the first monastery in the town of Rajgir, which became a centre of learning under the Gupta kings 600 years later. By the time the Chinese sage, Hiuen Tsang, came here in the 7th century, it was a thriving university for teaching philosophy, logic, grammar, medicine and Buddhist theology. It also sent missionaries to spread Buddhism to Tibet and attracted scholars from China, Burma, Thailand and Cambodia. It was destroyed by the Muslims at the end of the 12th century and the monks fled to Nepal and Tibet.

According to the Chinese traveller and and pilgrim Hiuen Tsang, the university in Nalanda had 1,500 teachers and 10,000 students, all on scholarships funded by the 'endowment' of 100 villages in the area. But getting in was not a piece of cake. Entrance examinations were exactly that: you could not get past the entrance of the university before answering a difficult oral question on philosophy, posed by the gatekeeper. Only about 10 percent got through the gate.

The museum has a good model of the original university and its monastery buildings, worth studying before you go out to the site. It also has a fine collection of bronzes from the 9th to the 12th centuries. On the excavation site, you will see remains of dormitories in addition to the refectory, kitchens, baths, lecture halls, libraries and temples.

THE SOUTH

This section takes in the states of Tamil Nadu, Kerala, Karnataka and Andhra Pradesh. The great sights of India's south include Mamallapuram, the ancient port of the Pallava kings, the abandoned city of Hampi, the wonderful Hindu temples and shrines of Madurai and Kanchipuran, and Sravanabelagola, with its 1,000-year-old giant statue of the Jain saint Gommatesvara. You can also immerse yourself in the bustle of Chennai, Bangalore and Hyderabad, and seek tranquillity in the mountains of the Western Ghats or the tropical backwaters of Kerala.

Travelling between Delhi, Mumbai and Kolkata, it's easy to forget that southern India exists. The attitude of northern Indians tends to be rather disparaging towards this part of the country, but a tour of the peninsula reveals a bright and cheerful people with a culture as rich and varied as their greener landscapes – the beautiful Malabar and Coromandel coasts.

The Dravidians who make up most of the southern populations don't mind being seen as different from northerners, but they don't want to be disregarded. Archaeologists can trace their origins to the builders of the first cities, Harappa and Moenjo Daro, in the Indus Valley. Their religion included elements of Hinduism such as Shiva's phallic lingam and his sacred bull, Nandi, before the Brahmanic Indo-Aryans arrived.

A Lamani woman, Hyderabad

Driven south, the Dravidians remained not only geographically separate, but also politically independent, impervious to the waves of foreign invaders.

Since Hindus battled Muslims until the end of the 16th century, they were by no means united. The Hoysalas of Karnataka, the Cheras of Kerala, the Cholas, Pandyas and Pallavas of Tamil Nadu all fought among themselves until the kingdom of Vijayanagar (Hampi in Karnataka, *see page 193*) emerged as dominant in the 14th century. Each of these kingdoms showed cultural vitality, exporting temple-builders together with their spices and ivory to Burma, Malaysia, Cambodia and Java. Suffering less than the north from the ravages of Muslim iconoclasts, their temples have survived in profusion and in much better condition. Today Madurai, Thanjavur (Tanjore), Belur and Halebid are principal custodians of the peninsula's ancient art treasures, while Bangalore is in the vanguard of India's modernisation, and Chennai, though without the self-promotion of Mumbai, produces as many feature films.

The strong regional identity of the south has repeatedly foiled attempts to spread Hindi and make it the national language here. On the east coast they point out that Tamil literature is much richer than that of Hindi. On the west, the people of Kerala, who speak Malayalam, boast the highest literacy rate in the country: 90 percent for the whole state, compared with 81 percent for the next highest (the district of Mizoram); and this with a national average of just over 57 percent.

Much better served by the rains, with some parts benefiting from the peninsula's two monsoon seasons, in the summer and early winter, the south's vegetation is luxuriant and colourful. There are coconut groves on the Malabar west coast, palmyra palms on the Coromandel east, and in between, a more barren landscape of rugged mountains and dramatic rocky outcroppings, relieved here and there by a patch of 'Flame of the Forest' trees, hibiscus or deep green jungle, as well as plentiful trickling streams, lotus ponds and lakes covered with scarlet lilies.

Chennai (Madras)

Chennai, known until 1996 as Madras, is India's fourth-largest city (pop. 7,000,000) and the gateway to the south of the country. The city is hot and congested, but the **beach**, an amazing 12km (7 miles) long, provides some relief (even though you can't safely swim from it).

Chennai was established in 1642 as the East India Company's first east-coast trading station for shipping cotton and sugar. After the defeat of the French, it took a grateful back seat in Indian affairs, far away from the turmoils of northern India. These days, fiercely independent-minded Tamil politics make the place much more lively and alert at election time.

Fort St George, where Robert Clive toiled as a young clerk when he first came to India, is nowadays the home of Tamil Nadu's State government and the Indian Navy. There is a **Military Museum** and a British 'relic' inside the fort: **St Mary's Church**, in the style of Wren. The most picturesque street in the

Downtown Chennai, complete with Victorian architecture

old town, across the railway tracks north of the fort (an area once known as 'Black Town'), is **Armenian Street**. Still the centre of a small Armenian community, it has a busy street market and, in a cool, tree-shaded garden, an open-air colonnaded church.

The **State Government Museum**, situated on Pantheon Road, possesses excellent Chola bronzes and a detailed collection of Dravidian sculpture and architecture. From 9th-century Pallavas and Cholas to the rich style of the Vijayanagar kingdom (1336– 1565), the exhibits make a fascinating demonstration in bronze and stone of the glory of South India. Foremost among its treasures are the **Amaravati Marbles**, fragments from the Amaravati Stupa which was all but destroyed by excavators in the early 19th century. The bas-reliefs, which outshine even those of Sanchi *(see page 140)*, are widely regarded as the high watermark of ancient Buddhist art in India.

The two main arteries of the city are the busy shopping centre along Anna Salai and Kamarajar Salai, where you will find the university, cricket club and **San Thomé Cathedral**. This simple, even austere, neo-gothic Catholic church houses what is claimed to be the tomb of St Thomas *(see below)*.

Doubting Thomas?

When Jesus sent his disciples around the world to spread the Good Word, the disciple Thomas was told to go to India.

'Whithersoever thou wilt, Lord, send me', said Thomas, as it is written in the Apocryphal Acts of the Apostles, 'but to India, I will not go.' Then, Gondophernes, a Pallava king on the northwest frontier, sent for a master carpenter to help with the building of a new city. Thomas' professional pride overcame his hesitant evangelistic fervour and he realised it was an offer he could not refuse. He converted Gondophernes and proselytised throughout the south, covering the Coromandel coast, where he is said to have suffered martyrdom — speared to death while praying in a cave in the southwest corner of modern Chennai.

Mamallapuram

The ancient port of the Pallava kings, a high point in any tour of south Indian monuments, is only 60km (36 miles) south of Chennai, but stay there overnight, rather than making a day trip from the capital, if possible. It has accommodation on the sandy beach, enabling you to see the carvings, *ratha* shrines and Shore Temple by the sea in the early morning and at night.

The town is named after King Narasimha Mamalla (630–68), 'the great wrestler', in whose reign its many extraordinary temples and shrines were begun. Like the cave-temples of Ellora *(see page 137)*, most monuments are

Arjuna's Penance at Mamallapuram

carved, rather than built, from solid rock, in this case the last rocky bluffs and boulders of the vast granite plateau that ends at the Coromandel coast.

South of the village is a set of *rathas*, monolithic shrines hewn from one table of rock. Imitating elements of the region's wood-and-brick construction, some have the same arched and domed roofs as the inner *vimana* sanctuaries that you can see at Thanjavur *(see page 179)* and at Srirangam *(see page 181)*. The largest shrine, the three-storeyed pyramidal **Dharmaraja**, at the southern end, has 50 figures, including gods, heroes and, fascinatingly, modest subjects such as temple servants.

Of the rock-carvings north of the rathas, the most celebrated is **Arjuna's Penance** (also known as Descent of the Ganga). The narrative sculpture panels cover an entire rock-face, in which a natural fissure has been assimilated as the Ganga River as it descends through the hair of Shiva.

The **Shore Temple**, which has withstood the wind and the waves for 12 centuries, is made up of two shrines, nowadays walled off from the corrosive breezes by a line of fir trees. Shiva the Destroyer faces dangers at sea while Vishnu the Preserver watches over the town. The temple, which would have served as a good orientation point for Pallava sailors, is clearly inspired by the styling of the monolithic Dharmaraja shrine, though more tapered.

Kanchipuram

Kanchipuram ('Golden City') has scores of temples – hundreds, if you include the shrines – dedicated to Vishnu and Shiva, and it is highly revered as one of the seven holy cities of ancient India. (The others are: Varanasi, Mathura, Hardwar, Dwarka and Ayodhya.) It's an easy trip of 70km (43 miles) from Mamallapuram and you can stop off to shop in Kanchipuram for silk.

Temple complex at Kanchipuram

Kailasanatha is one of the most important Shiva sanctuaries dating from the 8th century. The sandstone temple on a granite base houses some graceful sculptures of Shiva and Parvati as a celestial king and queen receiving homage from their subjects at their home on Mount Kailasa. **Vaikuntaperumal** is a Vishnu temple of the same period, famous for its elevated colonnade of lively sculpted reliefs showing the exploits of the Pallava kings.

Pondicherry

The most visible Gallic touch in this former bastion of the French colonial adventure in India is the scarlet képi worn by the white-uniformed traffic police waving you on as you drive into town. Many of the street names are still French – Rue Suffren, Rue Lauriston, Rue Dumas (Alexandre) and Rue Dupleix, now known as Rue Jawaharlal Nehru. However, only few people speak French here today. The French War Memorial on the coast road stands opposite a monument to Gandhi. After 250 years of French rule in Pondicherry, the Indians were fortunate to have the decoloniser Pierre Mendès-France to deal with when it was retrieved in 1954.

Apart from the pleasant white sandy **beach**, for nostalgics of the 1960s there's a pilgrimage to be made to the inspirational 'Mecca', **Auroville**. This utopian settlement, 10km (6 miles) north of Pondicherry, was started in 1968 by a Mira Alfassa, a Parisian painter of Egyptian-Turkish descent who was the spritual partner of the Bengali mystic-philosopher, Sri Aurobindo Ghose. Auroville lost some of its dynamism because of squabbles following the death of Alfassa, known to Aurobindo's acolytes as simply 'The Mother'. But the 'organic' forms of the buildings, with names like Hope, Fraternity and Aspiration, still have an impact on the landscape.

Thanjavur

Known to the British as Tanjore, this was the historic capital of the great Chola kingdom that spread Tamil culture to Myanmar, China and Southeast Asia. The extent of the influence of

**Temple of Brihadisvara,
Thanjavur**

its artful sculpture and architecture can be seen to this day in the temples of Cambodia, Thailand and Java. Commercial enterprise, military power and religious fervour went together. More than the divinity of Shiva, the architecture of the 11th-century **Temple of Brihadisvara** celebrates the victory of the great Chola kingdom over the Pallavas of Kanchipuram and the Cheras of Kerala. The accent is on the grandiose: the temple's main vimana shrine consisting of a massive, 13-tiered pyramid some 61m (200ft) high.

Shiva's sacred bull, Nandi, is built on a similarly colossal scale, as is the phallic lingam, believed to be the biggest in India. Frescoes insist (in gory detail) that head-chopping was necessary to achieve victory. However, a much more graceful architectural touch can be seen in the panels of Shiva demonstrating the 108 basic poses performed in the sacred dance, *bharatanatyam*.

Tiruchirapalli (Trichy)

The official, Indianised name of this town is Tiruchirapalli, City of the Sacred Rock, but the place is still identified by its colonial name, Trichy, a short form of the equally European name Trichinopoly. Today it is a base for pilgrims visiting Tamil Nadu's great temple complexes, but every schoolchild, at least those from the old school, knew Trichy for the British defeats of the French here in the 1750s.

The famed **Rock Fort** looms over the city from atop the great solid granite hill that gave the town its name. From early days, the impregnable rock served as a sanctuary, graced by temples and cave-shrines. Steep steps bring you up to the Hall of a Thousand Pillars, as well as the shrine of Shiva and the Temple of Ganesh, from which there is a fine view over the Kaveri (Cauvery) River, the towers of Srirangam and the plains beyond. On the way up, look for the 7th-century, stout-pillared Pallava cave-shrines.

The French legacy is discernable in Trichy, with the Jesuit College of St Joseph and the adjoining red-and-buff neo-gothic church of Our Lady of Lourdes.

Srirangam

The numerous temple precincts of **Sri Ranganathaswami**, set on an island formed by two arms of the Cauvery River 5km (3 miles) from Trichy, enclose a complete township of busy shops, booths and dwellings. Beyond the town's outside wall are the temple's farmland and the coconut plantations, and a large, square, lotus-covered bathing tank.

The temple itself, dedicated to Vishnu and already a theological centre by the 11th century, was founded a couple of thousand years ago – tradition takes it back to the Flood. Its present form comprises a total of seven concentric enclosures, culminating in an inner sanctum, and dates from the 15th and 16th centuries, after it had been liberated from Muslim invaders who had previously used it as a fortress. However, many of the sanctuaries are in fact much older than this.

Bathing at a temple festival, Srirangam

Enter on the south side and proceed through an ornamented *gopura* gate-tower characteristic of south Indian architecture. Next, pass under a series of soaring gopurams, where you can witness religion as a full-time daily occupation. The streets are crammed with vendors selling shrine offerings of sweets, curds and coconut, as well as garlands and holy images. Elsewhere, men are cleaning the stables for the temple elephants and the store-houses for the chariot-shrines that carry the deities through the streets during the festivals. Look out for the handsome pillared verandas of the dwellings.

On the south side of the fourth courtyard is the **Temple of Venugopala Krishnan**, with its charmingly sculpted figures in the famous Hoysala style of the temples at Belur and Halebid – notice the young woman with the parakeet, which served in Indian literature as a bearer of messages between passionate lovers. Non-Hindus can proceed as far as the sixth wall, but not into the golden-topped vimana, the inner sanctum, and its arched roof with the god Vishnu portrayed on each side.

Most spectacular of all, though, set in the eastern courtyard of the fourth enclosure, is the famous **Sesharayar Mandapa** (worship hall) with eight carved pillars of rearing horses bearing proud warriors. The energy of these minutely detailed sculptures from the 16th century, which honour the military prowess of the then-great Vijayanagar kingdom, is a zenith of south Indian art.

Madurai

The ancient capital of the Pandya kings and one of the world's oldest cities, **Madurai** is still an important repository of Tamil culture. Today it is a bustling university town, Tamil Nadu's second largest after Chennai.

The feverish religious activity around the nine towering gopuras of the **Great Temple**, 17th century in its present form, may give you a sense of the intensity of Hinduism. Its **Meenakshi Devi Shrine** is dedicated to a pre-Hindu 'fish-eyed goddess' taken into the pantheon with her husband, Shiva, whose **Sundaresvara Shrine** is next door. The Madurai festivals in April and May celebrate their marriage as a grand reconciliation with the Indo-Aryan invaders.

You can get a good overall view of the site by climbing the steps to the top of the **south gopura**. At ground level notice the arcaded **Golden Lotus Tank** and the bathing place. At the west end is a detailed model of the whole site.

The busiest place in the entire complex is the **Kambattadi Mandapa**, the ambulatory to the Sundaresvara shrine. Worshippers in procession prostrate themselves, bringing offerings of coconut and fruit, and toss tiny balls of butter onto blackened statues of Shiva.

The **Hall of 1,000 Pillars** (in fact only 997) is in the northeast corner of the complex. It is full of carved, bizarre lion-elephants, and the Pandava brothers, the heroes from the *Mahabharata* epic from whom the Madurai Pandyas claim descent.

Madurai's gopuras

Outside the eastern wall is the **Pudhu Mandapa**, the Hall of Audience of Tirumalai Nayak, the temple's builder. It is now a bustling bazaar with various artisans plying their trade.

Stop off at **Tirumalai's Palace**, about 1km (½ mile) southeast of the Great Temple. An elegant relic of former splendour, the palace boasts cusped arches and massive pillars modelled on the style of the great Rajput palaces of Rajasthan, but also some unmistakably tubby Dravidian gods on a frieze running around the courtyard.

Thiruvananthapuram (Trivandrum) and Kovalam

India's southernmost point is **Kanniyakumari**, where the Arabian Sea and Indian Ocean meet. There is nothing between you and Antarctica here. If your timing is right, you might get to see the full moon rising at the same time as the sun is setting.

A little further round the coast is the Kerala state border and then **Thiruvananthapuram**, the state capital. This is a sizeable place, and with its international airport is a popular transit destination for Indians and foreigners alike. Built on seven hills, it is named after the fabled serpent god, Anantha, on whom Sri Anantha Padmanabhan (Lord Vishnu) reclines. Created by the former rulers, the Maharajas of Travancore, Vishnu's temple still dominates the bustling old city. The Maharajas' heirlooms can be seen at their city residence, **Puttan Malika Palace**.

Just 15km (9 miles) south of Thiruvananthapuram is the popular beach resort of **Kovalam**, complete with coconut palms, papaya, bananas, white sand and surf (beware of the strong currents).

Varkala, 54km (32 miles) north of Trivandrum, is an attractive village and has a fine sandy beach at the base of cliffs. Watch out for fishing lines or nets that are dragged from the sea at around sunset. About 20km (12 miles) north of Varkala is **Kol-**

Cruising Kerala's Backwaters

In Kerala state, many tourists take the boats between **Kollam** (Quilon) and **Alappuzha** (Alleppey) along the picturesque backwaters. Two companies run the cruises: the state Water Transport Department boats are usually slower than Alleppey Tourism (the trip lasts up to 8 hours depending on the route).

At **Karunagapalli**, shipbuilders fashion *kettuvallam* (literally tied boats) out of jakwood planks sewn together with coir rope. Cruising *kettuvallam*, complete with rattan-thatched canopies, can be hired for two-day trips. Progress is often slower than by road as the waterways can be unexpectedly shallow and are often choked with waterlilies and duckweed.

Among Kerala's backwaters

lam, a cashew nut port which is the southern gateway to Kerala's famous **backwaters**. Travellers can journey through a network of narrow canals and wide lakes where people paddle to their daily tasks. Unlike the wave-tossed western seashore, which runs roughly parallel, the backwaters are calm. Boats of all descriptions are punted or sailed along the shallow green waterways.

Kochi (Cochin)

One of the most charming towns in India, where Christians, Jews, Muslims and Hindus live in much greater harmony than they seem to manage elsewhere, **Kochi** makes a delightful gateway to the Malabar coast and the relaxed life of Kerala.

On a peninsula separated from the mainland by islands, the old part of the town is known as **Fort Cochin**, where Pedro Alvares Cabral set up the first Portuguese trading post in 1500. Vasco da Gama also came here in the early 1500s, during the Portuguese campaign against the Zamorin of Calicut, further north. He was buried in the **Church of St Francis**, the only Portuguese building still standing here. It has been subsequently converted by the

Chinese dipping nets, near Kochi

Dutch to a Protestant church. The great navigator's remains were returned to Portugal in 1538 but his tombstone can still be seen on the south side of the church, set in the floor with a brass rail.

At the water's edge on the tip of the peninsula, you can see the fishermen's beautiful cantilevered **Chinese dipping nets**, a system imported from the China seas: fishermen sling the nets over a pyramid of four poles which is then lowered into the water and hoisted out again by a system of rock weights and pulleys.

The **Jewish quarter**, referred to as 'Jew Town', is in Mattancheri, south of the fort. In the narrow streets lined with merchants' and tailors' shops, the Star of David, menorahs and Jewish names are now more plentiful than Jewish people themselves. At Independence there were a few thousand, but when the State of Israel was founded, a massive emigration left only dozens behind. The synagogue, with its red tabernacle and Chinese tiling, was built in 1568. You can see the copper plates giving land rights to a Jewish community on the coast back in AD379.

At **Bolghatty Island** in the Kochi lagoon, visitors may take tea in the elegant Dutch governor's mansion, now a hotel.

Western Ghats

Inland, roads run due east and rise into the forest-covered **Western Ghats**. The road from Kochi leads up to **Munnar**, an old colonial hill station and the highest town in Kerala at 1,800m (6,000ft), surrounded by rolling hills with neatly clipped **tea gardens**. You can go wandering through the tea gardens at leisure, and there's plenty of accommodation locally. Nearby is the **Eravikulam National Park**, home of the endangered Nilgiri Tahr, the only species of ibex to be found south of the Himalayas, as well as elephants, gaurs, sambhar and lion-tailed macaques. This is also trekking country, dominated by the craggy **Anamundi**, the highest peak in southern India at 2,695m (8,842ft).

Wildlife enthusiasts should also make a point of visiting the nature reserve at **Periyar**, a drive of 194km (120 miles) from Kochi, via the busy Christian town of Kottayam. Here, elephants, bison and birds can be seen from the unique vantage point of an artificial lake. Look for the elephants with their trunks raised like snorkels.

Keeping the Faith on the Malabar

The first Jews arrived here from Palestine on the Malabar coast, at nearby Cranganur, in the early centuries of the Christian era. Far from Roman persecutors, they traded peacefully with the Hindus or with Arab merchants from the Persian Gulf. In time, their community was reinforced by new refugees from Babylon and Persia and then by others expelled from Spain and Portugal in 1492, spreading out along the coast.

However, the Portuguese settled there, too, bringing their Inquisition with them and upsetting the hitherto friendly Muslims. The Jews then promptly moved to Kochi, under the protection of the local Hindu raja. The Portuguese came down from Goa to smash the synagogue in 1662, but it was restored two years later. Today, with all but a few aged Jews resettled in Israel, there's no kosher butcher left in the town and little other trace of the Jewish population apart from their monuments.

Bangalore

Modern and efficient, the capital of Karnataka is a convenient gateway to the western half of the peninsula.

Under the former British Raj, Bangalore, at an altitude of 930m (3,000ft), was the summer refuge for its Madras-based officials, who with their parks and greenery had made it the 'garden city'. The spectacular growth of India's boom town in electronics, software, telecommunications, back-office and call-centre support has not only greatly increased the population (to over 6 million) but has noticeably changed the climate; it is several degrees hotter here now than it was 30 years ago. However, there are still pleasant walks to be had in **Cubbon Park** and in the terraced greenery of the botanical gardens of **Lalbagh**.

Mysore, the glory that was

Flanked by striking boulder hills of golden coloured basalt, the Bangalore–Mysore road provides a delightful introduction to the Deccan Plateau. Leading you along tributary streams of the Kaveri (Cauvery) River, past groves of mango trees, sugar cane fields and rice paddies, it is suddenly broken by the soaring mountain of solid granite which director David Lean made the location for the fateful picnic in his film of E.M. Forster's novel *A Passage to India*. You can visit Srirangapatnam and Somnathpur *(see page 190)* on the way.

Mysore

The home town of the maharajas regains a flicker of its former glory every October during the Dussehra festival, when the present Maharaja of Mysore State is paraded through the streets on his golden throne, surrounded by gorgeously caparisoned elephants *(see page 215)*.

Mysore remains a pleasant city, famous for its sandalwood and frangipani, jasmine and musk. The **Maharaja's Palace** is a museum by day and lit up at night, with the most striking decoration reserved for the annual Diwwali celebration. It was constructed in 1897 (after its predecessor was burned down) and represents all the excesses of Mughal nostalgia and undigested Victoriana. Doors of solid silver open onto the multicoloured, stylish décor of marble, mahogany and ivory. The highlight is an art gallery, with paintings of the maharajas in very British, landed-gentry poses, and a glass case featuring a 'rolled gold replica of the British crown' set next to a tea pot.

On the summit of the **Chamundi Hill**, the Sri Chamundeswari Temple offers a fine view of Mysore. On your way back down the hill, take a look at the massive black **Nandi** bull, Shiva's sacred vehicle *(vahana)*, with chains and bells that are a mixture of both real and sculpted items hung around its neck.

Another popular sight are the **Brindavan Gardens**, in Mughal style, some 19km (12 miles) north of Mysore, worth visiting at night when the fountains are flood-lit.

Srirangapatnam

The names of many southern towns are longer than their main streets. Situated due east of Mysore, Srirangapatnam was the site of the battles against the Muslim ruler Tipu Sultan in the 1790s, in which the British gained control of the peninsula.

The fort, which was taken by Lord Cornwallis and Colonel Arthur Wellesley (the Iron Duke with the rubber boots), no longer stands today, but the sultan's summer palace, **Darya Daulat Bagh**, has been preserved and made into a museum honouring the brave resistance of Tipu and his father, Haidar Ali.

Somnathpur

The **Kesava Temple** at Somnathpur, built in 1268, is considered one of the greatest examples of the Hoysala style. The structure is small, no more than 10m (30ft) high, and its vimanas (shrines) are set on a low, modest platform, but the temple achieves a grandeur in miniature, peacefully enclosed in its courtyard and isolated from the rest of the village. It is a tiny, shining jewel in the crown of Indian architecture.

The temple has been dedicated to Vishnu in his various aspects: as Janardana the Punisher, shown as a rigid, solemn-looking statue on the north vimana; as Kesava the Radiant, after whom the temple is named but whose statue is missing from the central shrine; and as Venugopala, the Krishna on the south shrine, with another Krishna (the cowherd) listening at his feet.

With a domed sikhara on each shrine, the temple's overall effect remains 'horizontal' in the style of the Hoysala kingdom, emphasised by the layers of narrow, parallel carved friezes running around the walls. Every square centimetre of the temple's surface is sculpted. An unusual feature in the Hoysala temples is that their carvings are signed by the sculptors. Like the statues of romanesque and gothic cathedrals portraying events from the Bible, the carvings were intended to be read like a book by those who had no access to the scriptures, which were at that time reserved for the Brahmins. They tell the stories of the gods – of the mischievous tricks of Krishna, as a child stealing butter from his mother and later as a young man stealing saris from girls bathing in the river – and of the adventures of the epic *Mahabharata*.

Belur and Halebid

The most comfortable way to see these important Hoysala temples is to visit them on either side of an overnight stay at Hassan, 120km (75 miles) northwest of Mysore.

The **Chenna Kesava Temple** in Belur is also dedicated to Vishnu the Radiant, but it was built in 1117, 150 years before the Kesava at Somnathpur. Legend has it that all Belur, Halebid and Somnathpur temples were designed by the same architect. The Belur temple's silhouette makes for an unfinished look, but it is not certain that towers or domes were ever planned. Here too, it is the sculpture rather than the form that gives the temple its impact.

The intricate carving of a huntress at Belur

The friezes bring the building to life with the legends of the gods, Shiva the demon-killer, or scenes from the *Mahabharata* including Prince Arjuna shooting a fish while looking at its reflection in an adjacent bowl of water. The bracket figures are masterpieces: a huntress, girls dancing or singing, and a woman about to spray her lover with rose-water. By the south doorway, on a vine chiselled beside the head of a girl dancing with a demon, you can find a lizard hunting a fly.

The **Hoysalesvara Temple** in **Halebid**, 16km (10 miles) from Belur, dedicated to Shiva and his wife Parvati, is the biggest of the Hoysala shrines. It suffered some destruction at the hands of Muslim iconoclasts, so it's worth visiting the **Archaeological Museum**, too, where some of the best of its statues are now kept. Look at the surprisingly fine carving of the bracket figures in the dancing hall, achieved by the craftsmen working with soft steatite soapstone which subsequently hardened to the texture of granite.

Sunflowers and coconuts near Halebid

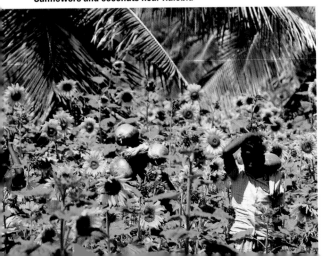

Sravanabelagola

Fifty kilometres (30 miles) east of Hassan, the Vindhya-giri Hill rises 140m (463ft) above the plateau, with one of the most dramatic monuments in all India, the statue of **Gom-matesvara**, on its top. To get to it, you must climb barefoot – the hill is holy ground – up 644 steps cut in the rock. Take it easy, and you will find the trip well worthwhile.

Statue of Gommatesvara

Erected in AD983, the statue crowns a sanctuary erected in the village of Sravanabelagola 1,400 years earlier by the Digambara sect of Jains, who regarded nakedness as part of the abnegation necessary to achieve true enlightenment *(see page 20)*. It is believed that in the 4th century BC Chandragupta converted to Jainism at Sravanabelagola and fasted to death.

Coming upon the statue at the top of the hill, even though you may have already seen it from a distance, is still an awe-inspiring experience. This Jain saint looms 17.5m (57ft) tall, carved from a granite monolith polished by centuries of libations with milk.

Gommatesvara, the son of the prophet Adinath, is entirely naked except for a single vine-creeper winding itself around his legs and arms. The creeper symbolises the impassiveness he is said to have observed in this upright position of *pratimayoga*, which he adopted for one whole year in response to his brother's lust for worldly power. An anthill and serpents at his feet symbolise the mental agony that his smile shows he had conquered.

Hampi

It was among the huge boulder-strewn landscape of the Deccan plateau that a pair of brothers, Harihara and Bukka, escaped the

> As well as being accessible from Bangalore, Hampi can also be reached from Goa by rail to the town of Hospet, half an hour from the ruins. The line running inland across the Western Ghats is now served by express trains, and the trip takes 8–9 hours.

clutches of the tyrannical Delhi Sultan Tuqhluq sometime in the first half of the 14th century and carved out for themselves an independent kingdom. Within 150 years, the rule of the dynasty they founded extended from coast to coast and to the tip of India. Vast riches poured in from the trade in horses and spices across the Arabian Sea, which successive rulers lavished on carved temples, palaces and a glorious city spread around the bend in the sacred **Tungabadhra River**.

The empire's unifying force was the common fear among its rulers of attack from the north by the Deccani sultans. With its vast standing army, Hindu Vijayanagar was a major obstacle to the Muslim kingdoms' territorial ambitions, so it was inevitable that sooner or later the two would come into conflict. The decisive battle eventually took place in 1535 at Talikota, in the no-man's-land buffering the warring kingdoms. It ended with the total destruction of what would prove to be India's last Hindu empire.

The ensuing sack of Vijayanagar lasted six months. By the end of it, the city whose grandeur had so impressed the Portuguese chronicler Domingo Paes in 1520 lay entirely in ruins, its inhabitants slaughtered, its temples, palaces and gardens burned to the ground and broken. Hindu pilgrims still come here to bathe in the river and worship at the Virupaksha shrine, whose gateway gopuras somehow survived the Muslim onslaught and still tower over the surrounding banana groves, visible for kilometres. For foreign visitors, the chief attractions of Hampi, aside from the wonderful archaeological remains, are the magical riverine landscape and surreal beauty of the boulder hills, which provide an exotic backdrop for bicycle rides and sunset walks around the ruins.

A view across Hampi

Visiting Hampi

Most visitors stay in the town of **Hospet**, 13km (8 miles) south-west of Hampi, which has a better choice of hotels and restaurants. From there it takes around half an hour to reach Hampi bazaar, whose western end is overwhelmed by the huge towers of the **Virupaksha Temple**. Follow the path leading from here along the riverside to the northern group of ruins, centred on the ornately carved **Vitthala Temple**. This is where you will see the finest examples of Vijayanagar's trademark 'rearing horse' columns.

You'll need to jump in a taxi to reach the southern, or 'Royal', group of monuments. En route, be sure to pull over half way to see the statue of Narashima – the huge, bulging-eyed depiction of Vishnu in his incarnation as the Man-Lion – which stands just off the roadside. Scattered over a wide area, the **Royal group**, a sprawling complex of palaces and ceremonial buildings, holds enough to keep interested visitors busy for days; in reality, the fierce Deccan heat is likely to limit how much you can take in at one go. Start at the **Mahanavami Dibba**, a massive pyramidal platform erected to commemorate a victorious military cam-

The famous stone chariot at Hampi

paign; its sides, and those of the nearby Kings' Audience Hall, are carved with rampaging elephants and mythological scenes. From there, work your way southeast towards the **Lotus Mahal**, where the queens and members of the *zenana* (harem) could relax in the shade of ornamental pavilions and domed corridors.

Finds from the archaeological site, including weapons, sculpture and palm-leaf manuscripts, are displayed at the ASI **museum** just south of the Royal group, alongside a scale model of medieval Vijayanagar which conveys just how vast and sophisticated the city was.

Bijapur

The powerful Bahmani dynasty formed the backbone of the Muslim military alliance that ultimately defeated Vijayanagar. This victory, and violent sack in 1535, provided the funds to endow their capital at **Bijapur**, northeast of Hampi, with a glittering crop of mosques, palaces and fortifications – collectively the finest display of Islamic architecture south of Agra.

Rising from the eastern fringes of town, Bijapur's *pièce de résistance* is the gigantic **Golgumbaz mausoleum**. The tomb dates from the twilight years of Bahmani rule and perfectly captures the spirit of a regime in decline: conceived on a ruinously grand scale, it exudes more self-importance than grace. All the same, it is an undeniably impressive spectacle. Capping the building, the vast free-standing dome is said to be the largest in the world after St Peter's in Rome.

At the opposite end of town – and architectural spectrum – is the **Ibrahim Rauza**, a gem of a walled tomb built on an altogether more human scale. Its appeal lies in its ornate décor, notably the famous pierced stone *jali* windows cut in the form of Qu'ranic inscriptions, and slender minarets and cupolas, which provide cover for flocks of screeching parakeets.

Finally, on your way to the Ibrahim Rauza, a monument worth the short detour from Bijapur's western gateway is the **Malik-i-Maidan** ('Lord of the Plains'), a huge canon installed in the 16th century. It took 10 elephants, 1,000 bullocks and an army of men to haul it into place. Steps from the emplacement lead to a higher bastion from where you can enjoy a wonderful panoramic view over the town and surrounding countryside.

Hyderabad and Golconda

Hyderabad, capital of Andhra Pradesh, is India's fifth-largest city (pop. 6,100,000). It dates from 1591, when Mohammed Quli of the Qutb Shahi dynasty moved his capital here from nearby Golconda. In 1687 the Mughal Emperor Aurangzeb

Working in the paddies near Hyderabad

overthrew the dynasty and appointed a viceroy, whose descendants ruled as the Nizams of Hyderabad until 1949.

The city's most famous landmark is the 1591 **Charminar** ('four towers'), a magnificent square archway supported by four 56m (184ft) towers. Nearby stands one of the largest mosques in India, the black granite **Mecca Masjid**, said to have bricks made of red clay from Mecca over the central archway. Surrounding the Charminar are bazaars with narrow cobbled lanes lined with rows of shops selling spices, tobacco, grain, perfume oils and Hyderabadi specialities. There is also a pearl market.

Golconda Fort

A visit to the former capital of the Qutb Shahi dynasty, **Golconda Fort**, 11km (7 miles) west of Hyderabad, is an easy daytrip and can be reached by local bus or auto-rickshaw. It was used by the last of the Qutb kings in the 17th century as a bastion against Mughal attack. Situated on a steep hill, the fort was encircled by immense walls with 87 semicircular bastions and eight gates with elephant-proof spikes. The remains of its once splendid palaces and gardens give an idea of its former grandeur. Diamonds and rubies once embellished the walls of the Queen's Palace, and rose-water filled a copper fountain.

Tirupati

In the south of Andhra Pradesh, Tirupati, with nearby Tirumala Hill on which stands the Lord Venkatesvara Temple, is the busiest pilgrimage site in the world, as well as one of the wealthiest. The very efficient temple administration employs around 16,000 people to deal with the 60,000-plus pilgrims a day who come for *darsan* (a view of the god). Many of them shave their heads as a pledge, or to thank the deity. The hair is used to make wigs, which are sold locally and exported. The temple is open to non-Hindus, but they must sign a form declaring their faith in god and respect for the temple's procedures. The steep road up the hill, with 57 hairpin bends, is not for the faint-hearted.

WHAT TO DO

SPORTS

One thing the Indians enjoyed about the British was their enthusiasm for sports – hockey and cricket in particular. In return, the British learned the delights of polo (imported with the Mughals from Persia and Afghanistan). Today, sporting life in India is still very active. Delhi especially has very modern facilities. The latest craze to hit the Indian sporting scene is Formula 1 motor racing.

Outdoor Activities

Be careful to adapt your activities to the climate, and avoid going out in the midday sun.

Swimming is a natural first choice. Many first-class hotels in leading cities have swimming pools, but there are a few precautions you should take when swimming elsewhere. For health reasons, it is best to avoid swimming in rivers, ponds, lakes and reservoirs – your body is unlikely to be able to deal with some of the other things swimming around with you.

Beach swimming is best at the recognised resorts rather than at the major port cities. In Mumbai, for instance, both Juhu and Chowpatty beaches are definitely a bad idea, and though the Marina beaches in Chennai are cleaner, there is a deadly undertow. The best resort beaches are on the Malabar coast at Kovalam and Goa. On the east coast, try Puri, south of Kolkata, or Pondicherry.

Wildlife can be enjoyed in India's 70 or so national parks and 330-plus sanctuaries. Among the most famous are Corbett, Kanha and Ranthambore national parks (for tigers), Gir Forest (for Asiatic lions), Periyar Wildlife Sanctuary (for elephants) and Eravikulam National Park (for the endangered Nilgiri Tahr, a type of ibex).

Ganesh immersion, the conclusion of the Ganesh Chaturthi Festival, in Mumbai

Hiking, or trekking as it is most often called here, is a marvellous way of getting away from the often madding crowd in India, and you will find it is well organised in the regions of Ladakh, the Kullu Valley (Himachal Pradesh) and Garhwal (Uttaranchal). Other trekking hot spots in the east include Sikkim, where you can walk to Kanchenjunga Base Camp. In the country's southwest, the hill stations of the Western Ghats near the Kerala-Tamil Nadu border are good bases for short treks.

Travel agencies happily provide a range of camping and cooking equipment, as well as the guides, cooks and porters you need, and a jeep for travelling to more remote and inaccessible areas. The necessary arrangements can easily be seen to on the spot, but a more ambitious six- or seven-day trek needs some notice, so it would be best to book with your trav-

A Passion for Cricket

Wherever you go in India, you'll see groups of youngsters engaged in a game of cricket. The Indians are passionate about the sport, and they play it wherever they can: in the backstreets, on the beaches, in the parks; in fact on any piece of flat ground where cricket could be played. Their knock-about games are keenly contested, and whether bowlers or batters, budding street talents have always wanted to emulate their heroes in the national side: heroes of the past, like Gundappa Viswanath, Kapil Dev and Sunil Gavaskar; and those of the present, like Sachin Tendulkar, Saurav Ganguly, Rahul Dravid and Anil Kumble. There is little chance of talent being recognised in the streets, however. Most cricketers who end up playing at the top level have much more privileged backgounds, coming from the wealthy, educated élite.

The Indians share their love of cricket with their neighbours, the Pakistanis, and sporting encounters between these giants of the game have always engendered the most passionate emotions of all. Amid the thaw in relations between the two countries, the rivalry on the pitch has helped cement friendships off it, and cricket, as well as being the national passion, has worked diplomatic wonders.

el agent and settle the details before you leave home. A quick search on the Internet will reveal dozens of Himalayan trekking specialists.

Spectator Sports

The most beloved sport in India, by far, is cricket. There is something in the intricacy of its arcane rules and controlled passion that appeals to the Indian people. It is an astounding obsession, and all major cities have stadiums. The most fervent atmosphere of all can be experienced at the Eden Gardens Stadium, home of the Kolkata Cricket Club, founded in 1792, just five years after the Maryle-

Kolkata race course

bone Cricket Club in London. The Wankhede Stadium in Mumbai is almost as intense for test fixtures. If you don't catch a major match, you may come across a competition in a Kolkata alley or a meadow in the mountains.

Hockey is a British import, in which the Indians have surpassed their former masters. Today they often share the Olympic finals with their old arch-rivals, Pakistan.

Polo is a Rajasthani speciality, but tournaments are also held in Delhi and Mumbai during the winter months. This is a rich man's sport.

Horse racing is popular, with races such as the Kolkata Derby, St. Leger, and the Oaks in Mumbai. The highest course in the country is at Darjeeling. Camel racing is a big event at Jaisalmer in February and also in the autumn festival at Pushkar *(see page 215)*.

Wedding dancers in action

ENTERTAINMENT

Music

Music of South Asia differs between the north and south, urban and rural environments, and men and women. The music most commonly associated with India in the West is that of the North Indian concert stage (known generally as Hindustani music), whose genres have their roots in the Muslim and Rajput courts. However, South India has its own concert traditions (known as Karnatic music), also in part stemming from the music of the southern courts, but also owing a great deal to a strong tradition of devotional song.

The concert music of South Asia uses a basic collection of seven pitches *(svara)* within an octave – *sa*, *ri*, *ga*, *ma*, *pa*, *dha*, *ni*, *(sa)* – which roughly correspond to the doh, re, mi etc. of Western music, and also have upper and lower ('sharp' and 'flat') variants. However, they differ radically from Western pitches by not having a fixed value, i.e., *sa* is fixed at a convenient level (higher or lower) for each individual musician, to suit an instrument, or his or her voice. Also essential to both Hindustani and Karnatic music are the twin concepts of *raga* and *tala*.

Raga (Sanskrit 'colour') designates which pitches it is permissible to play during the performance of a piece, and also (as different *ragas* share the same collection of pitches) characteristic phrases, 'ornamentations' as well as – although this is now less common – the time of day at which individual *ragas* should be played. This is particularly true of north India; in the south, concepts of *raga* tend to rely much more on the classification of different collections of pitches. Often misrepresented as merely a 'scale' or 'mode', a *raga* is more than a lineally arranged group of pitches (although this is often the most convenient way of notating them), but also implies the approach the musician should take towards the *svara*.

Tala (Sanskrit 'clapping') is the name for the repeating rhythmic cycles that underpin the metred sections of any Hindustani or Karnatic performance. Different *talas* consist of different numbers of beats (matra), and the first beat of a cycle, known in the north as *sam*, provides a reference point, not only for the musicians, but also the audience. At a performance of Karnatak music it is common to see the audience collectively marking the cycle through claps and waves on strong and weak beats respectively.

Playing the sitar

Khayal is the Hindustani vocal genre most commonly heard in the concert hall. A *khayal* composition (*bandis* or *ciz*) comprises two short sections, known as *sthayi* and *antara*, which are in contrasting registers. Usually two compositions are presented, the first in a slow tempo, known as a 'big' *(bara) khayal*, the

Learning the _vina_ in Kerala

second, a 'small' *(chota) khayal* in a faster tempo, which speeds up towards the end of the performance. A *khayal* concert starts with a short unmetred section introducing the *raga* (mode or pitch collection), followed by the *ciz*, which is in *tala* (rhythmic cycle), the most common of which is the 16-beat *tintal*. It is accompanied by the *tabla* (paired kettle-drums) and, traditionally, the bowed lute, *sarangi* (this is now usually replaced by the harmonium, a small hand-pumped organ that was introduced to South Asian music by French missionaries). The drone-lute *tambura* provides a constant background, sometimes played by a supporting singer and usually tuned to *sa* and *pa* (roughly corresponding to the Western doh and soh). The compositions are explored in a series of elaborations and improvisations.

Although sharing similar basic concepts of *raga*, *tala* and *svara*, Karnatic music differs quite considerably from the concert music of the north, perhaps most evidently in its performance of fully composed pieces, a lesser degree of improvisation and an important tradition of devotional song. Also, Karnatic music has tended to be a Brahmanical tradition, as opposed to that of either the Muslim or lower-caste musicians of the north. Karnatic music is overwhelmingly oriented towards vocal performance, especially with its emphasis on devotional texts. Vocal forms often included in concerts include the *kriti*, *varnam*, *kirtana* and *ragam-tanam-pallavi*. The latter form, in contrast to the devotional *kirtana* and *kriti*, stems from the musical traditions of the south Indian courts and is considered a great demonstration of technical skill.

Local performance traditions in India are usually associated with life-cycle and calendrical rituals, and also village festivals, often for local deities. Births, deaths and weddings are all accompanied by music, particularly by women singing. Marriage processions are usually accompanied by bands, traditionally playing oboes and drums, but now more commonly by brass bands playing covers of film songs. Funerals have traditionally been accompanied by low-caste drummers. Music and dance also accompany festivals such as Holi and the yearly Ganapati puja. At other times people gather in temples to collectively sing *bhajan* (devotional songs).

Film Music

The Indian music with the largest audience is *filmi git* (film song). The first Indian 'talkie', *Alam Ara*, was made in Mumbai in 1931. Following the conventions of traditional theatre, the action was broken up by songs and dances that served to push the action forward and represented the passing of time. These early films gained great popularity, and, as a consequence, so did the songs.

The singers in the early films were the actors and actresses themselves, but when recording technology allowed the songs to be dubbed in the late 1930s, most songs became pre-recorded, and specialists, known as playback-singers, took over. By this time, film song had become phenomenally popular, and playback singers became musical superstars.

The most popular, and enduring, of all playback-singers is Lata Mangeshkar. She, her sister Asha Bhosle, and singers such as Geeta Dutt, perform in a high-pitched style, very different to the lower, richer voices of the singers of the 1930s, and this has now become the dominant female film music vocal style. Popular male singers include Mohammad Rafi and Mukesh.

Screen idols Sri Devi and Sanjay Dutt

In south Indian temples, processions of the deities are accompanied by the *periya melam* ensemble of *nagasvaram* (oboe) and *tavil* (barrel drum).

Film

Film in India, produced mainly in the cities of Chennai, Mumbai, Kolkata and Bangalore, is a major industry. The large-scale production of entertainment films is a cultural phenomenon. You may well be more baffled by the appeal of the colourful musical comedies and violent shoot-em-ups than you would be in the West, but the emotion of the melodramas and romantic adventure stories of India's cultural and historic past have considerable curiosity value for a rainy afternoon. If you watch the action closely, you can learn a lot about Indian people by what makes them cheer, laugh or weep. Kolkata and Thiruvananthapuram seem to be the only other production centres having any pretensions to art cinema at all, but ironically you're actually more likely to see the works of Satyajit Ray or Mrinal Sen shown in Europe or North America than in India itself.

SHOPPING

From the Greeks to the Turks and Mughals, from Marco Polo to Lord Mountbatten, all have been seduced by India's riches. It is still a great place to shop.

Traditional craftwork continues to be produced at the highest level of skill: silks, carpets, jewellery, perfumes, brassware and wood-carving are first class, and you will have the added bonus of dealing with the most charming bunch of merchants in the world.

At least half the pleasure is in the bargaining. If you don't want to be fleeced, don't plunge in blindly. Go first to the Government Cottage Industry Emporiums, which can be found in almost every major city. The selection here is not usually as wide as you'll find in the privately run shops and you can't haggle, but it will give you an idea of the range of goods, the quality and, above all, the correct price.

Then you're ready for the fray, either in the bustling great bazaars such as Delhi's Chandni Chowk or Mumbai's Bhuleshwar, or the more sedate ambience of grander shops and showrooms. The one street market you shouldn't miss is Mumbai's Chor Bazaar, or Thieves' Market, which is an extravagant flea market where, among other things, you'll see Indian motorists buying back spare parts stolen from their cars the night before, or so the urban myth goes; the market is actually more famous for repro/fake antiques.

If, during your tours of the big cities, you come across products you like from places you will be visiting later, such as Rajasthan, Varanasi or Kashmir, wait until you get there – the price and selection may be much better.

Haggling with dapper Gujaratis and the bright-eyed Kashmiris can attain the level of high art. Even if you don't land a bargain, there is real aesthetic pleasure in seeing, at the end of the verbal 'combat', the disarray of silks thrown across a counter or a mound of carpets on the floor. Fleeing the insurgency war and dearth of tourists in their homeland, Kashmiri handicraft vendors have fanned out to tourist centres across India. Carpets and papier mâché are their traditional wares, but they also sell artefacts made by Tibetan refugees.

If there is no magic formula for the perfect bargain – each person will have his or her own psychological approach – you should avoid two extremes: don't be too eager, and don't, on the other hand, assume everybody is out to cheat you. It spoils the sport.

Carpets are one of the most attractive purchases you can make. Ever since the days when the Mughal Emperor Jahangir took Persian craftsmen up to Kashmir with him during his long summer holidays, the handwoven silk-and-woollen carpets of

Srinagar have been among the best in the world. The silk gives the carpets their unique sheen. The prices will vary according to the proportions of silk and wool used and the density of the weave itself; naturally, none of these pieces are cheap.

Look out for traditional Persian and original Kashmiri motifs such as peacocks and fruit trees, tiger hunts, and Mughal lovers. Indeed many of the carpets seem just too lovely to walk on, but they make superb wall hangings, and even if you can't remortgage your house to buy a big one, a modest bedside rug can do wonders to warm and brighten a room.

Cashmere, often in the form of 'pashmina', is a shawl of soft, warm wool shorn, you will be told, from the underbelly of the

wild Himalayan sheep. 'Shahtoosh' is the finest Kashmir wool of all, taken from the throat of the ibex and woven so finely that one can pass a shawl right through a wedding ring. These, too, are expensive, but you can get shawls of good quality wool with distinctive embroidery at more reasonable prices.

Silks have long been basic to a fine Indian woman's wardrobe and also make magnificent tunics, blouses, stoles or long scarves for a Western outfit. The costume more easily adapted to Western tastes than the sari, perhaps because it involves trousers, is a long tunic worn over baggy pantaloons with a stole around the shoulders; known as salwar kameez, it is most ubiquitous in the northwest.

Textiles are often embellished by embroidery

Three towns are famous for their silk: Bangalore, for its classic printed silk; Varanasi, for its gold and silver brocades; and Kanchipuram, for its heavy, brilliantly coloured silk, favoured for formal saris. Not forgetting the men, the city of Kanchipuram also produces superb silk ties.

Cottons, either hand-printed or embroidered, are probably the best bargain of all Indian textiles, made into tablecloths, napkins, bed linen, spreads, pillowcases and airy, light scarves that make life much more comfortable in the Indian heat. Indian tailors are cheap, good and fast, so you might consider having lightweight shirts and baggy pants made up for you during your stay.

Three cotton prints to look out for, particularly in Rajasthan, are: *bagru*, consisting of geometric or fish, almond and vine patterns in blue, brown and maroon; *sanganeri*, block printed floral and paisley patterns; and *bandhani*, tie-dye, which results in decorative colour. The bright motifs with mirror-work stitched into them, much favoured by Rajasthani women of the desert for their long flowing skirts, are known as *kutchi* or *saurashtra*. The dashing, rather coarse cotton Punjabi *phulkari* shawls are made from fabric with patterns in orange, pink, green, red and yellow.

Jewellery is important here, whether made with precious or semi-precious stones. The jewellery of Rajasthan is much sought after. Indian diamond mines produced some of the world's greatest gems, including the Kohi-nur (Mountain of Light), now in the British crown jewels, having originally been set in the Peacock Throne. Although the mines are superseded by those in South America and South Africa, the art of cutting and polishing is still extant in Gujarat. Mumbai is a centre for importing rough-cuts and selling the finished product. Don't buy any unless you are an expert or have one with you. Diamonds are graded from D to X, with only D, E and F considered good, D being colourless or 'river white', J 'slightly tinted', Q 'light yellow' and S to X 'yellow'.

However, the essential pieces of jewellery in India are the bangle and the simple golden chain necklace. Whole stalls are

Shopping in the bazaar

devoted to bangles, made from silver and gold, metal, wood, glass, plastic and – best bargain of all – colourful varnished papier mâché from Kashmir.

Gold, silver, copper and brass – each has its own bazaar in the big neighbourhood markets of Delhi, Mumbai and Kolkata. Of these, the most well known is Jains' Zaveri Bazaar in Mumbai, where antique gold is sold.

Wood carvings vary from rosewood elephants or sandalwood camels to the Kashmiris' finely fretted walnut, created in the style of the screens on the Srinagar houseboats.

For modern painting, try the art galleries around Connaught Place in New Delhi and Mumbai's Jehangir Gallery, not to forget the Academy of Fine Arts in Kolkata.

Spices are available in many markets around the country. If you want to take some home, where possible it's best to buy them in their whole form to preserve freshness. Tea enthusiasts will make a beeline for Darjeeling, to purchase directly from the plantations or at the town bazaar. When you take a couple of kilos, they'll ship it for you in air-tight packages.

Festivals and Fairs

In a country with such a strong and varied religious tradition, there is always some reason for celebrating something. Here is a selection (the dates are moveable because India follows a lunar calendar; precise dates around the time of travel are available through any tourist office):

January: *Pongal*, in Trichy and Madurai. A three-day harvest festival during which cows and bullocks are fed with rice, this is a celebration of the prosperity associated with the harvest. The atmosphere is generally jolly; the highlight is a variation on the bullfight in which young men try to pluck rupee notes from the horns of a very angry bull.

January 26: *Republic Day*, Delhi. Great march in which India shows off its cultural diversity and military might.

January/February: *Vasant Panchami*, throughout India but best seen in Kolkata. Honouring Sarasvati, goddess of scholars and artists; everyone dresses up in bright yellow and flies kites. *Desert Festival*, Jaisalmer. A lively celebration of Rajasthani music and dance, plus camel races in the local stadium.

February/March: *Carnival*, Goa. A hint of Portugal mixed with India; costumes and dancing in the streets. *Shivratri*, Khajuraho and Varanasi. Solemn celebration of Shiva, with all-night music and prayers in the temples. *Holi*, northern India, best at Mathura. The spring festival when IIndians spray each other with coloured powder and water.

March/April: *Gangaur*, Udaipur and Jaipur. Procession of girls balancing brilliantly polished brass pitchers on their heads with which they bathe Shiva's wife Parvati (Gauri); the garlanded deity is then accompanied by Shiva at the head of a parade of horses and elephants.

April/May: *Spring Festival*, Srinagar. Kashmiris bring out their samovars for a big tea party to celebrate the first almond blossoms, highlighted by mid-April festivities in the Mughal Gardens. *Baisakhi*, all over north India. The

Hindus' solar New Year. The Sikhs celebrate the anniversary of Guru Gobind Singh's exhortation to form the *khalsa* ('army of the pure').

June/July: *Rath Yatra*, Puri. One of the greatest festivals of the year, when the three gigantic temple-chariots of Jaggannath, his brother Balabhadra and sister Subhadra are drawn through the streets *(see page 167)*.

July/August: *Amarnath Yatra*, Kashmir. During the full moon, thousands of pilgrims make their way from Pahalgam to the cave of Amarnath to Shiva's ice-stalagmite lingam.

September/October: *Dussehra*, Mysore, Delhi and Kolkata. Ten days of pageant; elephant processions following behind the Maharaja of Mysore's throne; in north India, there is music, dance and drama centring in Delhi on the legendary hero Rama (with fireworks blowing up his demon enemy Ravana), and in Kolkata on the goddess Durga.

October/November: *Pushkar Fair*. Camels, horses and bullocks are brought to market. The camel races are spectacular, and this is a fine place to buy Rajasthani craftwork. *Diwali*, all over India. The happiest of festivals honouring Lakshmi, goddess of prosperity (except in Bengal, where they honour their goddess Kali, immersing her in the Hooghly River).

November: *Sonepur Cattle Fair*, near Patna. On the banks of the Ganga, this month-long cattle and elephant market is one of the world's biggest, bringing all the usual colourful eccentrics into town.

December 25: *Christmas*, Mumbai, Goa and Kerala. A more religious observance than in most Western countries.

Variable dates:
Muharram, Lucknow. Muslim mourning for Imam Hussein, grandson of Mohammed. Spectacular illuminated bamboo and paper replicas of the martyr's tomb are paraded through the town.
Id-ul-Fitr, Lucknow, Delhi and Kolkata. Mosques are lit up as Muslims celebrate the end of the Ramadan fast.

EATING OUT

India's fine cuisine is as rich and diverse as its civilisation – and home-cooking is best. However, big hotels and first-class restaurants will allow you the opportunity to taste various regional specialities.

The dishes are highly seasoned, but the spices are subtle; it will take some time for you to get used to the flavours, even if you're familiar with Indian cuisine back home. Although hotels are at pains not to overdo the hotter spices, it's still likely to be much sharper than you will be used to. So, take it easy – a little at a time. Indian food is fantastic and diverse everywhere, even in small provincial towns. Don't be afraid to taste local dishes (provided they're served hygienically). It's unlikely that you came to India to eat the same food that you're used to back home. In any case, Indians are much better at cooking Indian food than they are at preparing what the menu calls 'Continental' (i.e., bland all-purpose Western meals). Other than in Goa, few hotels break the beef taboo to serve steaks or hamburgers, though you may find some made from buffalo meat.

Breakfast

In large hotels, all the trimmings of British and American breakfasts are usually available: porridge (oatmeal), cereals, eggs and bacon, with tropical, fresh seasonal fruits such as mango, papaya and pineapple, and their juices.

Coffee in north India is usually instant, but do ask for the excellent South Indian filter variety wherever it's available. Tea is rarely Darjeeling, but you'll find the Assam type is as good as any in British hotels. For safety's sake the milk (which more often than not comes from buffalo rather than cows) is boiled, then re-cooled for the cereals.

The typical North Indian breakfast is a pile of hot *chapatis* or *parathas* with spicy fillings and a side portion of cold set yoghurt. In the south, you'll find favourites such as *dosas* (pancakes made of rice and lentils), *idlis* (steamed rice cakes) and *vadas* (fried doughnuts made of lentils), served with firey bowls of sambar broth and coconut *chatni*.

Lunch and Dinner

If you have plenty of things to do in the afternoon, keep lunch light and plan your main meal for around 8pm to give yourself enough time to digest. Hotels will often provide large buffets, giving you a chance to try several dishes, which people tend to pile up on one plate around a large mound of rice. But traditional Indian meals are served on a *thali*, a large metal platter, with each dish in

A fine Mughlai spread

a separate little bowl, *katori*, so that you can savour the different tastes separately.

Places that have assimilated the British custom will serve a soup like mulligatawny, which is a spicy chicken, mutton or vegetable broth created for colonial officials. Otherwise, with the exception of the food served at great banquets, meals are not divided into courses; everything will usually arrive on your thali at the same time.

You will find it good to follow the Indian custom of drinking something either before or after, but not during, a meal. Drinking does not in the end alleviate a peppery flavour because it will leave your taste buds completely defenceless against the next hot mouthful. Therefore, it's better to eat some plain rice or one of the soft Indian bananas, or, best of all, yoghurt flavoured with mint.

Spices in the bazaar

Indians eat with their fingers, rotating the fingertips around the plate to form the food into a ball with rice or bread. Cutlery may be provided, but a fork is not necessarily any more hygienic than fingers.

'Curry'

Properly speaking, there is no such thing as a curry. It's a British term invented to refer indiscriminately to India's spicy preparations of fish, meat and vegetables. It probably derives from the *karil* leaf common in southern cooking; an alternative theory is that the term comes from the copper *karai* dishes in which Mughal cookery is traditionally served.

In India there is not one 'curry powder' or 'curry sauce', because each dish has its own spices. The combination commonly used in a basic mixture of sautéed onions and garlic is called *garam masala*, a powdered blend of coriander, cumin, ginger, black pepper, cinnamon, chilli, cardamom, bay leaves, cloves and nutmeg. Saffron adds its own unique colour and fragrance, both to rice and to meat.

Non-Vegetarian

The classical cuisine of the north, *mughlai*, comes from the Mughals. With beef taboo for Hindus and pork for Muslims, the meat is lamb or mutton, its classic 'curry' being *rogan josh*. Cubes of meat are prepared in a yogurt sauce made with chilli, ginger, coriander and garam masala. This dish originated in Kashmir, where they eat lamb in dozens of different ways (if you attend a *wazwan* banquet, there may be as many as 16, 36 or even 52 dishes.).

Other dishes are the *kebab*, balls of lamb minced with almonds and spices; *tabakmas*, mutton ribs with a crispy skin; and *goshtaba*, the most tender lamb from the breast, with every last sinew beaten out of it before it is minced into a fragrant dumpling stewed in yoghurt. In Kashmir this is the climactic dish of a wedding banquet after eating the liver, the kidneys, the shoulder, the leg and various minced kebabs.

Biryani is a Mughlai speciality, originally exclusively a lamb dish, though chicken, fish and vegetables are now cooked in the same way. This dish is more elaborate than *pulao*, which is a simple mixture of rice and lightly flavoured meat or vegetables. Biryani is chicken or lamb cooked in a sauce of ginger, cardamom, cinnamon and cloves, before steaming it with saffron

The Spice of Life

You may be pleased to know that, according to the ancient canons of Indian medicine, the myriad spices in your meal are all working to improve your health. While the combination stimulates the appetite and helps your digestion in this very special climate, some of the individual spices have surprising properties.

Turmeric is very good for skin ailments, ginger for your liver and rheumatism. Cloves can help the kidneys, relieve fever and also stimulate the heart. Coriander fights constipation and insomnia, but one of the most versatile is cardamom, battling bad breath, headaches, throaty coughs and haemorrhoids.

Making chapatis

rice and *ghee* (clarified butter). It may be served decorated with almonds and mint and with a thin film of edible but tasteless silver, which adds luxury to the dish.

Chickens tend to be scrawny, but they are tasty in a *makhni* butter sauce as *murg ilaychi*, marinated in yoghurt with cardamom, ginger, peppers and saffron, or *murg do pyaza*, with shallots and onions. *Tandoori* chicken is a popular barbecue in the northwest style, baked in a *tandoor* clay oven. Typically, the chicken is salted and doused in lime juice, tenderised with papaya, then marinated in yogurt with a flavouring of ginger, garlic, chilli and saffron, before being plunged on a spit into the charcoal-heated oven.

Fish and giant prawns, marinated in different sauces, also make very good tandoori dishes. Fresh seafood is widely available, particularly from the kitchens of Goa.

Rice and Chapatis

The best rice is the aromatic long-grained basmati, the common or garden variety known as *patna*. Apart from biriani and pulao, north Indian cuisine does not feature large quantities of rice as does south Indian cuisine. The Indians in the north prefer to eat their food with a variety of breads, including a floppy, thin *roti* or *chapati*; a slightly thicker *paratha*, sometimes stuffed with vegetables or minced meat; small deep-fried *puri*; or giant puffed-up *nan*, baked in a tandoor. Here's a tip: before you tackle the rice dishes of the south, try eating with your fingers in the north by folding a piece of roti around each morsel.

Vegetarian

Favourite vegetable dishes, or *sabzi*, are *aloo gobi* (cauliflower and potato), *bhaingan bharta* (roasted eggplant), *sag panir* (spinach with Indian soft cheese), *bhindi* (okra), *channa* (chickpeas) and *dal* (lentil soup).

The cuisine of southern India is more vegetarian than that of the north. This is because the region was not subject to the Mughal influence. Whereas the north cooks with the products of its cattle, such as ghee for frying, yoghurt for sauces, and milk for desserts, the basis of southern cooking is the coconut – its oil is used for frying, and the milk and flesh for sauces. This gives the food a sweeter taste than in other regions. Sauces, in which water, palm vinegar or coconut milk is added to the spices, are gradually absorbed by the rice as the meal progresses.

Side Dishes and Snacks

Salads don't exist in the Western sense, but *cachumbar* is a refreshing side dish of tomato and onion seasoned with fresh lemon juice or vinegar. The great palate-cooler, eaten both in the north and south, is *raita*, a

India's strictest vegetarians exclude fish, meat, poultry and eggs, and even blood-coloured vegetables such as beetroot or tomato, quoting the ancient Sanskrit verse: 'In the next world animals will eat those who eat them in this world'. Some Brahmins of Bengal do eat fish, calling them 'fruit of the sea'.

mixture of cold seasoned yoghurt and either cucumbers, potatoes, tomatoes or pineapples.

As a sweet condiment, Indians serve not only mango, but mint and coconut, fresh ginger, tomato, dates or even tamarind in a spicy *chatni*. You'll find that some of the flavours in these dishes pack an astonishing double punch of sweet and sharp.

There are some wonderfully tangy Indian snacks. Mumbai's best is the *bhelpuri* sold on Chowpatty Beach *(see page 133)*, a spicy snack made from fried puffed rice, flavoured with tamarind juice, chillies and other spices. *Samosas* are stuffed with meat or vegetables, and *pakora* is a vegetable fritter. *Pani puri* is a small pastry stuffed with spiced tamarind water, so you should put the whole thing in your mouth at once.

Desserts

Ras malai are patties made from cottage cheese and nuts, sweetened with aromatic syrup, and perfumed with rose water and cardamom.

Goa for Gourmets

This former Portuguese colony, with a large Christian community, holds a unique position on the country's gastronomic map. Happy to use pork and beef in its very spicy 'curries' and pungent sausages, it also makes splendid use of the abundant seafood available off its Malabar coast.

Tisryo is a delicate dish of tiny stewed clams, spiced with ginger and sprinkled with coconut. But Goa's most celebrated dish, the 'Goan curry', is a thick sauce of tamarind, coconut, onions and tomatoes, served over a variety of local seafood such as clams, prawns, crab and anything else the fishermen have caught that day, all of it spiced to the gills. Known in English simply as 'fish curry', it's eaten twice each day by working Goans. You probably won't have room for an *alebele*, a sweet and spicy crêpe stuffed with coconut. But if you do, eat it with with *feni*, a potent spirit distilled from either cashew fruit juice or partly fermented palm sap.

Cashews and *feni* in Goa

Khir, rice pudding, invented in India with condensed milk and broken rice, mixed with cardamom and nuts, is far superior to its British counterpart. *Gajar halwa,* a dessert of grated carrots stewed in milk and syrup, is best hot, with raisins and nuts. *Kulfi* is ice cream made with cardamom and pistachio. *Barfi* and *halwa* are sweets made with flour or milk and flavoured with nuts and fresh cardamom.

Drinks

The most cooling drinks are *nimbu pani* (water with fresh lime) and fruit juices, especially from the fragrant Kashmiri apple. Indian beers are acceptable, wines (produced in the hills outside Bombay and Pune) drinkable, and whisky tolerable.

Imported New World wines are very expensive and, frankly, not good to drink with Indian food anyway. Among traditional Indian alcoholic drinks are palm toddy in Kerala; *chang,* a barley beer from Ladakh; and a rose- and opium-based liqueur made in Rajasthan. In Goa people drink *feni* (*see opposite*).

HANDY TRAVEL TIPS

An A–Z Summary of Practical Information

A

ACCOMMODATION

Indian tourist accommodation caters to all tastes. There are luxury hotels in big cities as well as in all major centres of tourist interest (such as Agra and Jaipur). In former princely states, maharajas' palaces have been converted into hotels, those in Rajasthan being very successful. Some have been taken over by large companies; others are run by members of princely families. There are numerous smaller but comfortable establishments at much lower rates throughout the country.

Most hotels will ask you whether you want 'AC' rooms (air-conditioned) or 'non-AC'. From May to September it is wise to spend a few rupees more to enjoy a cool retreat. Be wary of the water in the plastic flask near your bed. In the cheaper hotels, check your bed linen and do not hesitate to have it changed if necessary. Officially, foreigners are expected to pay their hotel bills in foreign exchange. However, this is only really applicable to luxury establishments, since few others have access to the day's rate of exchange.

YMCA and YWCA hostels (couples, married or not, are accepted) are in every large town and provide adequate, often excellent, accommodation. Most railway stations have **rest rooms** where you can stay for a night or a few hours. They are clean and cheap; you must hold a valid railway ticket to qualify for one.

A great way to get to know India is to stay with an Indian family. Such **home stay** accommodation is organised in Rajasthan, Kerala, Ladakh, Chennai and Mumbai in alliance with the Tourism Development Corporations of the respective states.

AIRPORTS

The international airports in Delhi and Mumbai welcome the bulk of tourists and visitors to India. Airports at Kolkata, Chennai and, in the south, Thiruvananthapuram, Cochin, Kozhikode and Hyderabad, are also equipped to receive international flights.

Indira Gandhi International Airport, New Delhi, is located 20km (12 miles) southwest of the city. The terminal facilities include a buffet and a number of currency-exchange counters, as well as a luggage deposit facility, duty-free shop, and hotel reservation, car-hire and pre-paid taxi counters.

Chhatrapati Shivaji International Airport, Mumbai, is situated 29km (18 miles) north of the city centre. This is by far India's busiest airport, both for international and domestic services. Its international terminal (formerly Sahar), which is based over 5km (3 miles) away from the domestic terminal (formerly Santacruz), but linked to it by a regular shuttle-bus service, has all the facilities of a modern airport. At peak hours, the journey from the centre to the airport can take 3 or more hours, so allow for transfer time.

ALCOHOL

Only one state in India, Mahatma Gandhi's home state of Gujarat, remains completely 'dry'. Alcohol is generally available elsewhere, except in very remote areas and in religious centres. The once compulsory All India Tourist Permit is no longer necessary. Some hotels will ask you to drink either in your room or in the hotel's licensed bar – but it's up to you to shake off the guilt complex. Other than luxury hotels, few restaurants are authorised to serve beer or other alcoholic drinks.

ARRIVAL (see also CUSTOMS, ENTRY AND EXIT REGULATIONS)

On arrival you will be required to fill in a Disembarkation Card. These are generally distributed to passengers on board the plane. Visitors who do not have any dutiable goods, high-value articles, foreign exchange in excess of US$1,000 or unaccompanied baggage, all of which have to be declared, can simply walk through the Green Channel. However, others will have go to the Red Channel for the appropriate clearance.

Ground transport. Airport terminals are organised to provide you with a cheap bus ride into town at regular intervals, and throughout the night if the airport is a busy one. Airport bus services can be found in smaller places. You are also assured of finding taxis – usually from well organised 'pre-paid' booths where you purchase the ticket at fixed fares in advance. Elsewhere, a policeman at the gate will ask for your name and destination (he isn't prying, he is simply curbing taxi-driver greed). Destinations and current fares are posted on a large board.

Departure. Security checks at airports are particularly intensive in India. Check in at least 3 hours ahead of departure time for international flights, and 2 hours in advance for domestic ones.

B

BUDGETING FOR YOUR TRIP

The following are some prices in Indian rupees and US dollars. However, they must be regarded as approximate, due to inflation.

Car hire. Remember that all hire cars are chauffeur driven. In the cities a car may be hired on a flat-rate basis (e.g. 4 hours or 40km Rs200 non-AC; Rs300 AC). For travel outside the cities, count on around Rs1,000–1,200 for up to 80–100km, and Rs 8–10/km thereafter. More will be charged for a luxury imported vehicle than for an air-conditioned (AC) Indian car. Overnight charges for the driver start from Rs150 to Rs250 per night.

Discover India Pass (Indian Airlines). US$400 for 7 days, US$630 for 15 days, US$895 for 21 days.

Hotels. Double room in a luxury establishment Rs3,000 to Rs10,000 per night. Middle-of-the-range hotels from Rs1,000 to Rs1,700 per night for a double, depending on whether it is air-conditioned or not. Local and luxury taxes are extra, approximately 5–20 percent, although this can depend on the state in which you are travelling.

Indrail Pass (Indian Railways). US$270 for 7 days, US$495 for 30 days, US$1,060 for 90 days, first-class AC. Other periods available.

Meals. A snack: Rs50 upwards in a budget restaurant; from Rs250 in a luxury hotel. Full meal (Indian style): from Rs150.

Taxis. Fares to and from airports and major train stations are supposed to operate at a fixed rate. Elsewhere, the driver should agree to use the meter but the usual compromise is to agree a fare for the journey before you get in.

Trains. Delhi to Mumbai (approximately 1,400 km/1,000 miles) AC first-class Rs2,834; non-AC couchette Rs401.

C

CITY TRANSPORT

Taxis exist in all large cities. **Tourist cars** (chauffeur-driven) can be hired in centres of tourist interest through the local tourist office. Drivers should agree to use the meter, converting the reading at the end of your journey with a 'rate card'. However, they may be reluctant to do so and in practice it's easier to haggle a fare in advance.
Motor-rickshaws, also known as scooter-rickshaws or autos (three-wheel mini-taxis), operate in a similar way. Again, fare rates vary from town to town; in general, a scooter-rickshaw fare is about half a normal taxi fare. Always fix fares in advance, which may involve haggling. Scooter-rickshaws are banned in Mumbai's congested inner-city zone (and from the airports), so you must use a taxi, bus or suburban train.

In all big cities there is an efficient **bus** service which, when you know how to use the route guide available from all bookstalls, is convenient. The only problem is that buses in India carry large crowds and are not always well driven.

There are also **cycle-rickshaws** and *tongas* (horse-drawn carts), for which you agree on the price before starting off. Kolkata and Delhi have **metro** lines (both are clean and cool).

CLIMATE

India can be conveniently divided into three zones – the north, the south and the hill regions – and into three distinctive seasons: the winter, the summer and monsoon. The best time to vist India is from mid-September to early April, except for the hill stations, which are good at any time in the summer except during the monsoon.

The monthly average maximum and minimum daytime temperatures* in degrees Celsius are:

		J	F	M	A	M	J	J	A	S	O	N	D
Mumbai	max.	28	28	30	32	33	32	29	29	29	32	32	31
	min.	19	19	22	24	27	26	25	24	24	24	23	21
Kolkata	max.	27	29	34	36	36	33	32	32	32	32	29	26
	min.	13	15	21	24	25	26	26	26	26	24	18	13
Delhi	max.	21	24	31	36	41	39	36	34	34	34	29	23
	min.	7	9	14	20	26	28	27	26	24	18	11	8
Chennai	max.	29	31	33	35	38	38	36	35	34	32	29	29
	min.	19	20	22	26	28	27	26	26	25	24	22	21

And in degrees Fahrenheit:

		J	F	M	A	M	J	J	A	S	O	N	D
Mumbai	max.	83	83	86	89	91	89	85	85	85	89	89	87
	min.	67	67	72	76	80	79	77	76	76	76	73	69

		J	**F**	**M**	**A**	**M**	**J**	**J**	**A**	**S**	**O**	**N**	**D**
Kolkata	max.	80	84	93	97	96	92	89	89	90	89	84	79
	min.	55	59	69	75	77	79	79	78	78	74	64	55
Delhi	max.	70	75	87	97	105	102	96	93	93	93	84	73
	min.	44	49	58	68	79	83	81	79	75	65	52	46
Chennai	max.	85	88	91	95	101	100	96	95	94	90	85	84
	min.	67	68	72	78	82	81	79	78	77	75	72	69

* Minimum temperatures are measured just before sunrise, maximum temperatures in the afternoon.

COMMUNICATIONS (see also OPENING TIMES)

Telephones. India boasts a modern, efficient telephone system. From virtually any street corner (look for the yellow signs advertising ISD/STD Telephones) you can make long-distance and international calls, whose durations are accurately recorded to the nearest second on meters. Once you hang up to finish the call, a printer produces a ticket outlining the length of your call and its cost. Expect much higher charges than you may be used to in your home country. Rates vary according to the day and time, being most expensive in office hours and cheapest at weekends and between 10pm and 5am.

Note that many telephone businesses will offer a 'call-back' facility, allowing you to receive calls from someone once you've phoned to tell them the number. This will save money as it invariably works out cheaper to dial India from abroad rather than the other way around.

Internet and Email. For a huge country where telephone charges are relatively high and postal services unreliable, the Internet has provided an inexpensive and popular means for people to keep in touch, and as a result you'll find 'Internet Booths', cafés and computer terminals in all but the most remote villages. Most places these days are equipped with fast ADSL or broadband lines. Rates vary from state to state, from around Rs40 per hour to Rs75.

Postal service. The postal service within India and abroad is generally slow and unreliable. An airmail letter usually takes up to 10 days to Europe or the US. Stamps are sold at post offices and in some large hotel receptions. It is best to watch your letters being franked rather than using public letter boxes. Lower denomination stamps and envelopes tend not to stick very well, hence the pot of glue on all counters. You can send bulkier souvenirs home by surface mail, but you must first have the package cleared by customs. The Speed Post service for internal mail is quick (most letters are delivered within 24 hours), cheaper than a courier, and more reliable than standard post. This service is also available for sending letters and parcels to a few foreign countries (destinations vary from one post office to another). More reliable than the Indian postal service are international courier services, available in larger towns and cities.

CRIME AND THEFT

One wouldn't expect to recover a camera left on a park bench anywhere in the world, and India is no exception. However, your valuables are probably less at risk in India than in many parts of the West. Common-sense precautions go a long way: don't leave valuables lying around, and avoid being obvious – a few hundred dollars are a year's earnings to many people.

Violence against foreigners is not unknown in India, but it is probably safer to walk through Delhi late at night than many places back home.

CUSTOMS, ENTRY AND EXIT REGULATIONS

Visas. All travellers, including Americans, EU citizens and citizens from Commonwealth countries, need visas. For some strange reason, however, Polish travellers are exempt.

Entry visas apply to those frequently travelling to India on business assignments; they can be extended.

Transit visas, with a maximum duration of 15 days, are only needed if you are simply making a stop-over and want to leave the airport. They are granted to passengers who have tickets for onward destinations. Two-way transit visas can also be obtained.

Tourist visas are normally valid for six months. It's virtually impossible to extend a tourist visa – you have to travel to a neighbouring country and apply for a new one. You must arrive in India within six months of the visa date of issue, or it will automatically become void. For a tourist visa, you will need two passport-size photos. Unless you hold a passport from a fee-exempt country, you will be expected to pay for your tourist visa. Tour organisers can arrange for group visas.

Some parts of the country are designated restricted areas and require **entry permits**. See PLANNING YOUR TRIP for more details.

Arrival (see also AIRPORTS). Certain high-value items, such as laptop computers and expensive photographic equipment, may be entered in your passport by customs officials. Any items that have been written into a passport cannot be sold and must be shown on departure. In case of loss or theft, you will need a police document to prove that you have reported the incident. Firearms and habit-forming drugs are banned and so is the import of gold bullion and electronic items for commercial purposes.

Departure. When leaving, you are not allowed to take recognised antiques (items that are over 99 years old) – it is best to keep your sales receipt with you. You may not export any kind of animal skin other than a small amount of cow leather and a few peacock feathers. **Currency restrictions.** It is forbidden to take Indian rupees into or out of the country. There is, however, no limit set on the total amount of foreign currencies you can bring into India, providing you declare amounts in excess of US$2,500 on arrival. Foreign currencies that total the amount imported and declared may be exported.

E

ELECTRICITY

Power supply is 220V 50Hz AC, via two- or three-pin round plugs. European visitors should be able to run their appliances using a simple adaptor, widely available locally, while those from the US may also need a transformer. Supply can be erratic, particularly during the summer months, when air-conditioning units crank into life, massively increasing demand and leading to what is euphemistically referred to as 'power shedding' – power cuts by any other name. Supply is generally more stable at night.

EMBASSIES, HIGH COMMISSIONS AND CONSULATES

Most countries have diplomatic ties with India, with an embassy or high commission in New Delhi and a consulate in Mumbai, Kolkata or Chennai.

Australia	*High Commission*: 1/50G Shanti Path, Chanakyapuri, New Delhi 110021; tel: 26888223
	Consulate: Maker Tower, 'E' Block, 16th Floor, Cuffe Parade, Colaba, Mumbai 400005; tel: 22042044
Canada	*High Commission*: 7/8 Shanti Path, Chanakyapuri, New Delhi 110021; tel: 26876500
	Consulate: 41-45 Maker Chambers, VI, 4th Floor, 6 Jamnalal Bajaj Marg, Nariman Point, Mumbai 400021; tel: 22876028/29
New Zealand	50-N Nyaya Marg, Chanakyapuri, New Delhi 110021; tel: 26883170
	Consulate: 132 Cathedral Road, Chennai 600086, tel: 28112472
UK	*High Commission*: Shanti Path, Chanakyapuri, New Delhi 110021; tel: 26872161

UK	*Consulates*: Maker Chambers, IV, 1st Floor, 222 Jamnalal Bajaj Marg, Nariman Point, Mumbai 400021; tel: 22830517
	1 Ho Chi Minh Sarani, Kolkata 700071; tel: 22885172
	24 Anderson Road, Chennai 600006; tel: 28273136/37
US	*Embassy*: Shanti Path, Chanakyapuri, New Delhi 110021; tel: 24198000
	Consulates: Lincoln House, 78 Bhulabhai Desai Road, Mumbai 400026; tel: 23633611 and 23633681
	5/1 Ho Chi Minh Sarani, Kolkata 700071; tel: 22823611
	220 Annar Salai, Chennai 600006; tel: 28112000

G

GETTING THERE

Due to the complexity and variability of the many fares, you should ask the advice of an informed travel agent well before your departure.

Scheduled Flights

All major international airlines land at Delhi and Mumbai (see under AIRPORTS); some also fly to Kolkata and Chennai. Approximate flying times: London–Delhi 9–10 hours; New York–Delhi 17–18 hours.

Charter Flights and Package Tours

From North America: India is featured on a number of tours from the United States, many of them combined with another country such as Nepal, China or Japan. There are a number of package tours from Canada.

From the United Kingdom: Tours include air/hotel packages to Kolkata, Mumbai, Delhi, Goa, Jaipur, Kovalam, Chennai and Udaipur.

There are also tours that take in two or more Indian cities and that combine India with another country such as Nepal or Sri Lanka.

From Australia and New Zealand: India is sometimes featured on Asian tours, but these are not frequent.

Overland

It is possible to cross into India by land from both Nepal and Bangladesh, but the journey can be somewhat strenuous – by bus from Kathmandu to Dehli, or by bus from Dhaka to the Bangladesh border, then by train to Kolkata. Both routes take a minimum of two or three days. The border with Pakistan is often closed, and the bus service between Delhi and Lahore, though currently in operation, can be suspended without warning.

GETTING AROUND

Air (see also AIRPORTS). India has an extensive airline network. Don't waste time on arrival: book as soon as you know where you are going and how you want to get there. There are two types of ticket: *confirmed*, which are (mostly) trouble-free, and *requested* (or *wait-listed*), which frequently offer only a slim chance of travel.

Indian Airlines (IA; <www.indian-airlines.nic.in>), the state-owned domestic carrier, offers tourists discount *Discover India* fares, for 7, 15 or 21 days. Tourists are expected to pay for their tickets at a disadvantageous 'dollar rate'. In Delhi, the IA office is on Connaught Place, at F-Block, Malhotra Building; tel: 23310517. In Mumbai: Air India Building, Nariman Point, Mumbai 400021; tel: 22023031.

Well worth considering are the private airlines, notably Jet Airways (<www.jetairways.com>), which in most cases offer a smarter and more dependable service than the national carrier. In addition, a handful of competitive low-cost airlains has started up in recent years, including: Air Deccan (<www.airdeccan.net>); Kingfisher Airlines (<www.flykingfisher.com>); Spicejet (<www.spicejet.com>); IndiGo (<http://book.goindigo.in>); Sahara Airlines (<www.airsahara.net>).

Rail. Indian Railways (administratively divided into Northern, Western, Eastern, Central and Southern railways) have five basic classes of travel: First Class Air Conditioned (AC), Second Class AC, AC Chair, First Class non-AC and Second Class non-AC. During the summer months an AC compartment is best, especially if travelling through the Indian plains. Other than a few super-deluxe fast trains, there are three types of train: *Express*, *Mail* and *Passenger*. You should certainly avoid *Passenger* trains, which stop at every station no matter how long the journey.

All long-distance trains have sleepers. Third Class seats are wooden planks; First and Second Class and AC berths are cushioned. Second Class berths, whether AC or not, give straight onto the main corridor, but First Class berths are separate compartments with slide-doors and catch-locks. In First Class and Second Class AC, you are provided with sheets and blankets (nights can be chilly in AC, even in the summer).

Indrail Passes are available, abroad or in India, for various periods of up to 90 days. Tourists are expected to pay for their tickets in foreign exchange.

Since the introduction of a computerised reservation system, booking tickets has become a lot faster and easier. That said, you should aim to obtain your ticket as far in advance as possible. Major stations in Delhi, Mumbai, Kolkata and Chennai have dedicated Tourist Reservation Counters, which speed up the whole process considerably for those with foreign passports; tickets purchased at them always have to be paid for in foreign currency, with travellers' cheques or with cash backed by an encashment certificate from an Indian bank or ATM. Foreigners need their passports for booking tickets.

Bring plenty of books, fruit and water. You will marvel at the ability of Indian travellers to emerge from a 48-hour journey as fresh as when they started, while you will be in dire need of soap and water.

Food is served on Indian trains. However, apart from one or two luxury trains, there won't be much of a choice (generally it will be a question of vegetarian or non-vegetarian). Meals will consist of a thali or a cardboard box filled with plastic bags of curry and rice.

India also has a number of **special trains**. Indian Railways run two 'Royal Trains' – the Royal Orient and the Palace on Wheels – through Rajasthan and Gujarat, using luxury carriages with on-board catering; bookings can be made through travel agents in your home country. A train pulled by the world's oldest working steam locomotive, the 1855 Fairy Queen, makes a three-day excursion from Delhi to Alwar, taking in the Sariska Tiger Reserve; tel: (011) 23405156. Hill Trains India has a number of charming 'toy trains' which run from the plains up to certain hill stations, including the narrow-gauge tracks up to Ootacamund (Ooty) in the Nilgiri Hills, the line from New Jalpaiguri to Darjeeling, and the track between Neral and Matheran near Mumbai.

Road. Where there is no railway (e.g., parts of Rajasthan), there will be a road and dozens of inter-city buses. The fares are low, and so is the comfort. Buses on major routes are plush and classy. Discovering India by car is more comfortable, and cars are rented chauffeur-driven.

The best advice to anyone who is thinking about driving in India is: don't. Roads can be very congested and dangerous and there are many unwritten rules followed by other drivers. It is far better, and cheaper, to hire a car with chauffeur. However, if you do have to drive you will need your domestic licence, liability insurance, an international driver's permit and your vehicle's registration papers.

H

HEALTH AND MEDICAL CARE

Before travelling to India, you are advised to take out a personal health insurance policy to cover possible mishaps. Likewise, consult your family doctor for a routine check-up and ask him or her to prescribe medication for potential stomach upsets. Anti-malaria tablets must be taken at least two weeks before departure and for six weeks upon returning home. Remember also to pack a small bottle of light wound disinfectant.

Most people during the course of their stay in India will contract some form of stomach trouble. In most cases, it is nothing to worry about, being more irritating than anything else. The remedy is simple: avoid rich, spicy food for a while, double-check drinking water (be sure to avoid tap water), peel all the fruit you eat and take medication if required. Bottled mineral water is widely available in most towns and cities, but may be difficult to obtain in off-track districts. Stock up whenever possible. When bottled water is unavailable, purify your water with a chemical steriliser such as chlorine or silver nitrate, or else boil it for at least 4 minutes.

Due to the dramatic weather changes between seasons, people can catch heavy colds at any time of the year. Carrying tablets that combat flu symptoms will help. Dust may cause conjunctivitis, so eye drops will come in handy. Sensitive skin also needs to be protected against the sun. Bring insect repellent and an anti-irritant for insect bites. High levels of heat can cause outbursts of prickly heat (use talcum powder) and migraines. Take plenty of liquids to combat dehydration.

Although not mandatory, vaccinations against typhoid, tuberculosis, hepatitis and tetanus may be worth it. A valid yellow fever certificate is mandatory for those arriving from South America, Africa and other areas where yellow fever exists.

While in India, steer completely clear of stray mammals – particularly dogs – because there is a risk of rabies.

Cities like Delhi and Mumbai have Western-style clinics; your embassy in New Delhi can recommend one. Government hospitals are cheap, but not always as hygienic as those you might be used to at home, so if you are going to have injections done, insist that the doctor either uses a disposable needle or that the sterilisation process is carried out in front of you; this is for your own peace of mind.

L

LANGUAGE (see also USEFUL EXPRESSIONS)

Hindi, based on Sanskrit and akin to many European languages, is the official national language of India, but each state also has its own regional language – one of the 18 listed in the Constitution. English is still used alongside Hindi for official purposes.

People in north India generally speak Hindi, while in the south, where the regional languages are Dravidian, you will find more English spoken.

M

MAPS

Good road maps of the Indian subcontinent are published in Europe, and the Indian tourist offices in the US hand out useful maps and brochures.

Street maps are not always available, but your best bet will be the local tourist office or your hotel reception desk. Street maps of big cities like Delhi and Mumbai can be bought from newspaper stands.

MEETING PEOPLE

All transactions and most social encounters in India begin with the well-established ritual of exchanging visiting cards. Like everywhere else, politeness in India is considered to be a virtue. You'll quickly find that most Indians will go out of their way to be friendly and helpful to you. A traveller will frequently be asked about his or her nationality, name, marital status and children, though the limited spread of English tends to restrict the scope of most conversations to simple things. It can be a bit tedious to go around like a walking curriculum vitae, but just keep smiling. This quaint curiosity is built on the best of friendly intentions, and it is part of India's charm.

No topics of conversation are taboo, providing you don't take up an intransigent or arrogant stand. On the contrary, Indians are extremely eager to explain their country and their beliefs to foreigners, which could make for interesting conversation.

Indians increasingly shake hands when greeting people, especially during the course of official business; in formal situations a traditional *namasté* with both hands brought together at face level and a slight bow is considered polite.

Many Indians do not drink and/or are vegetarian, so if you are inviting someone out for a meal, it would be a good idea to inquire beforehand about tastes and preferences.

MONEY MATTERS (see also OPENING TIMES)

Currency. The Indian unit of currency is the *rupee* (abbreviated *Rs*), which is divided into 100 *paise*. There is a 50 paise coin, and coins of 1, 2 and 5 rupees. Banknotes exist in denominations of 2, 5, 10, 20, 50, 100, 500 and 1,000 rupees.

Indians are rather fussy about the condition of their paper notes. A shopkeeper often turns down a note because it is very slightly torn at the edge while accepting another one with a great big hole in the middle! There is a very much mistaken belief that the Reserve Bank of India has ruled that notes which are torn at the edge are worthless. In fact, the Reserve Bank has a special counter for accepting or exchanging torn or soiled notes, and most other banks will do the same. However, they may refuse to do so if you don't bank with them. So check your change carefully every time you pay for something, and refuse any frayed and dirty notes. Don't try to mend notes with transparent sticky tape – they become unacceptable this way.

There is a chronic shortage of small cash and many shopkeepers give out sweets or stamps by way of change. Taxi and motor-rickshaw drivers are also notoriously without adequate change; you might often find yourself having to pay a little more just to break up a roadside deadlock. When cashing in your foreign exchange in a large bank, it would therefore be a good idea to ask to have part of your Indian money given to you in small notes. Some banks give extremely valuable wads of small change. Hang on to the bank receipts, since you may well need them when booking train or air tickets. Note that it is a criminal offence to change money on the black market.

Travellers' cheques can be cashed in at most banks and in many hotels, though in the latter case it may be at a slightly inferior rate. Some shops are also authorised to deal in foreign exchange.

Debit and credit cards and personal cheques. Use and acceptability of debit and credit cards is becoming increasingly widespread in India now. All big hotels and government emporiums recognise them, and so do many shops and restaurants, while ATMs are attached to most banks. However, personal cheques will find few takers, although some foreign banks will help you out, providing you can produce a foreigner resident in India who will stand as surety.

N

NEWSPAPERS AND MAGAZINES

English-language newspapers, both national and regional, are widespread throughout the country. There is a large number of English-language news magazines, some of which are absolute musts for those interested in the intricacies of Indian political and social life. Most of the major cities now have a weekly *What's On* type of magazine (available from bookstalls), which gives the opening and closing times for museums and information on current cultural events.

O

OPENING TIMES

All central government offices, except post offices, railways, etc., follow a five-day week, closing on Saturdays and Sundays.

Most **markets** close one day a week; the day varies from place to place. **Shops** generally open at 10am and close by 8pm; some are shut for lunch.

Administrative **offices** (other than central railway and airline offices) only start becoming active by about 11am; they will be devoid of life by 5.30pm. The official lunch break is from 1.30 to 2pm. Station booking-counters open with the first trains.

Banks dealing with foreign currency open from 10.30am to 2.30pm on weekdays, and from 10.30am to 12.30pm on Saturdays. However, on Saturdays it may be difficult to change your travellers' cheques outside the main cities. There are ATMs in most towns and cities.

Post offices open at 9.30am, closing at 5.30pm in larger places and 3.30pm elsewhere.

Museums and **parks** are open until 5 or 5.30pm, but you should check which day they stay closed.

Hairdressers in large hotels will take clients in the early evening.

P

PACKING

While most things are easily available in large Indian towns, there are still certain items you'll be relieved to have with you.

Other than essential medicines (see HEALTH AND MEDICAL CARE), think of packing the following items: a pocket torch (flashlight); a padlock if you are thinking of staying in a few cheaper hotels (combination padlocks spare the worry of losing the key) or if you are going to travel a lot on Indian railways; a penknife (but don't try to board planes with it in your cabin luggage); a packet or box of wet wipes for freshening up and cleaning sticky fingers, water-purifying tablets; a money belt; and half a dozen passport-size photos of yourself, which will come in useful if you are applying for permits to restricted areas or for a rail pass. A universal plug for wash basins will come in handy more often than you might imagine.

Aspirin and mosquito repellent are readily available, but you might like to have your own favourite brands handy. Also, don't forget to pack some sterile cotton wool and adhesive bandages, and last but not least, toilet paper or paper tissues (found only in large Indian towns and tourist resorts).

Sewing kits can be useful, but in every hotel there will be somebody to do the job for you; if not, on every sidewalk there is at least one tailor or one cobbler capable of performing instant miracles for a few rupees.

Pack a cloth hat to protect against the sun, as well as sensible light cotton clothes to wear during the hot and monsoon seasons, a swimsuit, and a fleece top for cold spells during the winter months or trips to the hills (see also CLIMATE).

Ear plugs can sometimes be a life-saving device, particularly at night in crowded compartments, or in a bus with non-stop Indian film music (often distorted) blaring out of the public address system.

Finally, you might also like to bring with you a few small gifts for people who have been particularly helpful and shown you hospitality. Virtually any small item with a foreign trademark on it will be happily accepted; this could be football shirts, stamps from your own country, picture postcards, coins, etc. In many places you might find yourself surrounded by swarms of children clamouring for 'school pens and coins' – by ignoring their pleas you will help discourage such pestering.

PHOTOGRAPHY

Digital photography is fast becoming the norm in India, and you find photographic shops equipped with the latest card readers where you can upload and back up your images in most towns and tourist resorts. For a small fee they'll also burn the data on to discs. Colour and black-and-white print film is readily available in the main cities, but film for slides is not easy to find. Some shops in big cities do stock E6 preparations (Agfachrome, Fuji Sensia, etc.) but retail prices are higher than in Europe. Professional film stock is only available in the big four gateway cities.

Delhi, Mumbai and other cities and larger towns have plenty of photo studios that can process black-and-white or colour film. Generally the quality is good, but prints are usually postcard size only. It is perhaps best to take the film back home with you to have it processed there.

India is a colourful country, and your finger will be itching on the shutter trigger of your camera from the moment you arrive. However, there are certain things that cannot be photographed: military installations, bridges of all sorts, airports and railway stations, power stations and refineries, dams and telephone exchanges. Likewise, it is always best to get permission to photograph any person.

PLANNING YOUR TRIP

Most of India is open to foreign travel, but special permits have to be obtained to visit certain parts of Arunachal Pradesh, Mizoram, Nagaland, Manipur, Sikkim and some islands, including the Andaman Islands. (Assam, Tripura and Meghalaya, which once also required permits, are now open to tourists.) Some of these areas are open only to organised tours, not to individual tourists; time limits on visits also apply in some cases. Information on restrictions and permits should be obtained from your local Indian tourist office or Indian embassy in advance of your trip.

Though the government of India places no restrictions on travel in Kashmir, and local tour companies are busy enticing clients, most foreign consulates warn against travel in this region due to the ongoing political unrest. Kashmir should not be considered as a destination for tourism until the situation there has been resolved.

POLICE

Indian police have earned a reputation for being incorrigibly corrupt. As a foreigner, any dealings with the police – such as reporting thefts of valuables or a passport – are likely to involve requests for a small bribe – Rs100 rupees should suffice to oil the wheels. Should you be arrested for any reason, contact your consulate at the first opportunity.

PUBLIC HOLIDAYS

Due to the many religions in India, public holidays are plentiful and confusing. Fixed national holidays are set on the following dates: 26 January, Republic Day; 15 August, Independence Day; and 2 October, Mahatma Gandhi's Birthday. Banks are closed on 30 September and 31 March. Other holidays vary according to region. A list of official holidays can be obtained from tourist offices. *See also pages 214–5.*

R

RADIO AND TV

All India Radio (AIR) broadcasts on medium wave, with news either in English, Hindi or a regional language.

As well as the somewhat dull and dated government-run television stations, India hosts more than 150 satellite and cable channels, both local and international, which are available in most hotels. BBC World and CNN are invariably on offer, along with MTV and dozens of Bollywood channels.

RELIGIOUS SERVICES

No other country in the world has such a wealth of faiths as India, reflected in the religious activities of its people and the beautiful architecture of its churches, mosques and shrines.

Access to places of worship is generally open, except for some Hindu temples and all Parsi fire-temples. Mosques are closed to non-Muslims at certain times of day. In most places of worship you will be asked to take off your shoes and/or cover your head, so it might be a good idea to take along some form of head-covering. You'll find Sikh *gurdwaras* ban the entry of tobacco, while Jain temples forbid anyone entering the premises to bring in any form of leather (including wallets). Therefore, if you wish to take advantage of all the opportunities for sightseeing, you should consider packing a hip bag or money belt made from canvas or another fabric that would be acceptable.

Synagogues can be found in big cities such as Mumbai and Delhi; Christian churches of a variety of denominations exist in practically every town.

RESTAURANTS

First-class hotels naturally offer restaurants with sophisticated surroundings and a touch of luxury for the traveller. There is no foolproof way of sorting out the better restaurants before actually sampling the food. Trial is still the best method for judging standards. Many of the small roadside establishments, not exactly enticing by some Western standards of conviviality, sometimes serve excellent fare for next to nothing, but these are not recommended for the short-stay traveller.

On the Menu

aloo	potato
barfi	sugar and milk sweets
biryani	slow-cooked north Indian rice and meat dish

chai	tea
chapati	unleavened bread cooked on a pan or griddle
chawal	rice
dal	lentils or kidney beans
faluda	sweet noodles with milk and ice cream
ghosht	meat, generally mutton
halwa	carrot- or semolina-based dessert
idli	little dumpling of steamed rice flour, eaten at breakfast with chutney and curry
kebab	barbecued meat
keema	minced meat, generally mutton
kirra	cucumber
kofta	spicy minced-meat balls
korma	a curd-based curry sauce
kulfi	Indian ice cream
lassi	curd-based milkshake, sweet or salty
masala	mixed spices
masala dosa	pancake of rice flour and ground lentils with spicy potato filling
mutter	peas
nan	leavened bread
nimbu pani or nimbu soda	fresh lime with water or preferably soda
pakora	deep-fried savory fritter with onion or potato
paneer	Indian cottage cheese
papadum	crispy spicy wafers
paratha	flaky chapati, generally fried in butter and often stuffed
pomfret	type of very fleshy fish
pulao	north Indian rice and meat dish
puri	deep-fried 'bubble' chapati
raita	curd (*dahi*) mixed with either tomatoes, green peppers, cucumbers, potatoes or pineapple

roomali roti	paper-thin chapati
roti	generic name for oven- or pan-cooked bread
sabzi	vegetables
sag	spinach
samosa	deep-fried, stuffed pasties
seer	type of very fleshy fish
tandoori	meat (generally chicken) marinated in spice and curd, cooked in a traditional oven
tikka	pieces of diced meat/fish, marinated and grilled

S

SMOKING

Some states, notably Goa, have recently imposed a ban on smoking, though in practice this seems rarely enforced. The Sikh religion forbids smoking, so you will be asked to hand in all your tobacco at the entrance when visiting a *gurdwara* (Sikh temple).

T

TIME DIFFERENCES

Indian Standard Time (IST) is GMT plus 5½ hours, winter and summer alike. The most bizarre time difference in the world exists between India and Nepal: 15 minutes!

	New York	London	**Delhi**	Sydney
January	1.30am	6.30am	**noon**	5.30pm
July	2.30am	7.30am	**noon**	4.30pm

TIPPING

It is customary to leave a tip of about 10 percent of the total bill in restaurants. However, tipping elsewhere is entirely discouraged by the Government of India. Do not try to tip government employees, although museum guides will invariably give hints at the end of a conducted tour, so it will be up to you to decide whether his stories and information are worthy of a tip. However, in temples it's a different story: the baksheesh is more or less mandatory. You should also give a rupee to the person who looked after your shoes while you were visiting.

TOILETS

Despite improvements in recent years, the toilets in India are generally very, very basic, but all the same, don't shun the 'Eastern' (seatless) version, because they are often much more hygienic than the European style. The water tap nearby is to wash your bottom and hands.

TOURIST INFORMATION OFFICES

Indian tourist offices at the addresses below will help prepare your trip. The official website is <www.incredibleindia.org>.

Australia: Level 2, 210 Pitt Street, Picadilly, Sydney, NSW; tel: (02) 9264-4855

Canada: 60 Bloor Street (West), Suite No 1003, Toronto, Ontario M4W 3B8; tel: (416) 962 3787/88

UK: 7 Cork Street, London W1X 2AB; tel: 020-7437 3677/78

US: 1270 Avenue of the Americas, Suite 1808, New York NY 10020; tel: (212) 586-4901; 3550 Wilshire Boulevard, Suite 204, Los Angeles, CA 90010; tel: (213) 380-8855

In India the major tourist offices are:

Mumbai: 123 Maharishi Karve Road, opposite Church Gate; tel: 22033144/45

	Chhatrapati Shivaji Airport: Domestic tel: 28325331; International tel: 26156920
Kolkata:	4 Shakespeare Sarani; tel: 22825813. Dum Dum Airport; tel: 25118787
Chennai:	154 Anna Salai; tel: 28460285
	Meenambakam Domestic Airport; tel: 22340386
	Meenambakam International Airport; tel: 22345801
Delhi:	88 Janpath, New Delhi 110001; tel: 23320005
	Indira Gandhi International Airport; tel: 25696021
	Domestic Airport; tel: 25675181

Airport tourist offices are open 24 hours a day; others 9am to 6pm.

U

USEFUL EXPRESSIONS

Hindi is spoken mainly in the north of the country. Here are some useful words and expressions to listen out for and use. Verbs ending with a '-yé' sound are polite imperatives, but those ending with an '-o' are familiar forms of address. The '-ji' suffix is a polite honorific. A wavy line over a vowel indicates a nasal sound.

Yes	ji hā
No	nah
Please	meher bāni
Thank you	dhanyavād (sometimes 'shukriyā' in northern India)
My name is….	Mera nam…hai.
What is your name?	Apka nam kya hai?
Beg your pardon/sorry	māf (or shama) kijiyé
Hello/welcome/goodbye	namasté
How are you?	kyā hāl hai/āp kaisé hai
I'm fine.	thik haī

I don't understand.	samjhā nahĩ
Tomorrow/yesterday	kal (confusion is possible)
Today	āj
Tonight	āj rāt ko
This morning	āj subhā
This evening	āj shām ko
Good	achchā
Excellent/well done	shābāsh
Fast/early	jaldi
Slow/late	dhiré
Money	pāisā
How much is it?	kyā dām hai
It is very expensive.	yé bahut mahinga hai
Are you free?	kyā āp khāli hai
(taxi, rickshaw)	
How far is it?	kitni dūr hai
Where is it?	kahā hai
On your right	dãy
On your left	bãy
Straight ahead	sidha
Please stop here.	yahã rokiyé
Please go faster.	jaldi chaliyé
Please go slowly.	dhiré chaliyé
Please go away.	jãiyé
Go away!	jão
Let's go!	chalo (polite form chaliyé)
Please bring...	lãiyé
Please give...	dijiyé
I'm not feeling well.	mai kuchch bimār hū
I need a doctor.	mujko doctor chaiyé
This is not good.	yé achchā nahihai
It is very good.	bahut achchā hai
It is very hot.	bahut garam hai

It is very cold.	bahut thandā hai
It is very beautiful.	yé bahut sunder hai
Please give me some water.	mujko pani dijiyé
This is not clean.	yé saf nahi haī

The following two are fairly important since they are not only typically Indian but also occur in the press, and on official documents, etc.

100,000	lakh (written: 1,00,000)
10,000,000	crore (1,00,00,000)

NUMBERS

1	ek	12	barah
2	do	20	bis
3	tin	30	tis
4	char	40	chalis
5	panch	50	pachās
6	chhé	60	sāth
7	sat	70	sattar
8	ath	80	assi
9	nau	90	nabbé
10	dass	100	sau
11	gyarah	1,000	hazār

TAMIL EXPRESSIONS

Hello	vanakkam
Goodbye	poyvituvarukiren
Yes	amam
No	illai
Thank you	nandri
What is your name?	Ungal peyar yenna?
My name is….	Yen peyar….
Where is…?	…yenge?

INDEX